China's Pension System

Since 1978, when China started remaking its economy, it has also embarked on an unparalleled effort at remaking its pension system to accommodate its hybrid economic model. This book tells the story of how China has managed to build a national pension system that now covers most of its population and what this system holds for its future.

This book covers the following topics: evolution of Chinese pension system to its current form; benefit design, financing, and governance of current pension system; challenges facing the pension system, especially the looming funding shortage due to accelerating population ageing; solutions to the challenges; and lessons learned from the Chinese experience. Due to the fragmentation of pension system among 31 mainland provinces, we also select three provinces as case studies to help readers gain a richer understanding of how economic and geographic diversity has created disparity in pension benefit design and financing between provinces and within a province and how such disparity adds complexity and challenges to the pension system.

This timely and important study provides up-to-date and in-depth analyses for policymakers and stakeholders to make informed decisions and will be relevant for all scholars and students of public administration and public policy studies.

Jun Peng is Professor at the School of Government and Public Policy, University of Arizona. His research focuses on state and local government financial management in the U.S., and he authored "State and Local Pension Fund Management" which was published by Taylor & Francis.

Qiushi Wang is Professor at the Center for Chinese Public Administration Research and School of Government, Sun Yat-sen University. His research interests center on public budgeting and finance, and his articles have appeared in *Public Administration Review* and *Journal of Public Administration Research and Theory*.

Routledge Focus on Public Governance in Asia
Series Editors:
Hong Liu, *Nanyang Technological University, Singapore*
Wenxuan Yu, *Xiamen University, China*

Focusing on new governance challenges, practices and experiences in and about a globalizing Asia, particularly East Asia and Southeast Asia, this focus series invites upcoming and established researchers all over the world to succinctly and comprehensively discuss important public administration and policy themes such as government administrative reform, public budgeting reform, government crisis management, public—private partnership, science and technology policy, technology-enabled public service delivery, public health and aging, talent management, and anti-corruption across Asian countries. The book series presents compact and concise content under 50,000 words long which has significant theoretical contributions to the governance theory with an Asian perspective and practical implications for administration and policy reform and innovation.

Mainland China's Taiwan Policy
From Peaceful Development to Selective Engagement
Xin Qiang

Public Administration and Governance in China
Chinese Insights with Global Perspectives
Leizhen Zang and Yanyan Gao

The Nature of Japanese Governance and Seikai-Tensin in Postwar Japan
Nara Park

Managing the COVID-19 Pandemic in South Korea
Policy Learning Perspectives
Kilkon KO

China's Pension System
Creating Sustainable and Equitable Social Security
Jun Peng and Qiushi Wang

For more information about this series, please visit www.routledge.com/Routledge-Focus-on-Public-Governance-in-Asia/book-series/RFPGA

China's Pension System

Creating Sustainable and Equitable
Social Security

Jun Peng and Qiushi Wang

Routledge
Taylor & Francis Group

LONDON AND NEW YORK

First published 2024
by Routledge
4 Park Square, Milton Park, Abingdon, Oxon OX14 4RN

and by Routledge
605 Third Avenue, New York, NY 10158

Routledge is an imprint of the Taylor & Francis Group, an informa business

British Library Cataloguing-in-Publication Data
A catalogue record for this book is available from the British Library

ISBN: 9780367550981 (hbk)
ISBN: 9780367550998 (pbk)
ISBN: 9781003091974 (ebk)

DOI: 10.4324/9781003091974

Typeset in Times New Roman
by Apex CoVantage, LLC

Contents

Figures

Tables

Acknowledgments

This work was supported by the National Natural Science Foundation of China, 2021, Grant ID: 72174215, and the Major Program of Key Research Base of Social Science and Humanities, Ministry of Education of China, 2022, Grant ID: 22JJD630022.

Abbreviations

CASS	Chinese Academy of Social Sciences
CNY	Chinese Yuan
HRSS	Human Resources and Social Security Department
MOF	The Ministry of Finance
MOHRSS	The Ministry of Human Resources and Social Security
NCSSF	The National Council for the Social Security Fund
NSSF	The National Social Security Fund
PAYGO	pay-as-you-go
SOEs	state-owned enterprises

1 Overview

1.1 Introduction

Just like the meteoric rise of its economy since it implemented a "reform and opening" policy in the late 1970s, China has also made tremendous strides in establishing a nationwide pension system almost from scratch over the same period. This system now covers most people in the country. Along the way, through trial and error, China has created a pension system that shares some common features with the pension systems in other countries and exhibits some unique features that reflect its own historical, economic, and political roots. This book delves into these similarities and differences, as well as the challenges and opportunities facing the Chinese pension system in the 21st century as a result of these similarities and differences.

Why should a book on the Chinese pension system be of interest to scholars and students of public administration mostly living outside China? We offer a few reasons here:

- China is both the most populous country in the world with 1.4 billion people as of 2021 and one of the fastest-ageing nations in the world. It is also the second-largest economy in the world, accounting for 18.4% of world GDP in 2021, according to the World Bank (2022). This combination of demographics and economic size makes pension benefits and funding in China of considerable significance to the world economy in at least two ways: the pension can affect the size of workforce in China, as it can be affected by the normal retirement age, which currently is one of the lowest in the world; it will also affect the livelihoods of hundreds of millions of people, whose consumption will also constitute a very significant part of the Chinese economy in the foreseeable future.
- With trillions of dollars in pension assets to invest, it can also have an impact on financial markets, not just in China but worldwide as well.
- Last but not least, the similarities and differences in pension systems between China and other countries should also offer a rich case study on how a pension system can be developed, as well as its pros and cons, especially for other countries in the process of developing pension systems.

DOI: 10.4324/9781003091974-1

While this book is essentially a case study on the Chinese pension system, it is still worth comparing China to broadly recognized practices in establishing national pension systems in the rest of the world to understand the unique aspects of the Chinese pension system. This comparison involves three major aspects of the national pension system: the major components of the pension system, the coverage of the public pension component of the pension system, and how the public pension is funded and any related financing issues.

1.1.1   Three pillars of a national pension system

When considering what a national pension system should look like, it is useful to bring up the framework proposed by the World Bank (1994). An ideal national pension system should have three pillars:

- the first pillar is a government-sponsored national public pension plan that should cover every eligible adult in the country;
- the second pillar is an employer-provided occupational pension; and
- the third pillar is an individually financed personal retirement account on a voluntary basis.

The reason for this three-pillar pension system is to spread out the pension burden so that no individual entity, the government, employer, or individual, will bear a disproportionate burden of financing retirement benefits. This is also related to the concept of replacement ratio, meaning the percentage of a person's income prior to retirement that is replaced by pension. A replacement ratio indicates whether a person's quality of life can be maintained in retirement or not. While there is no consensus on what the exact replacement should be, it is generally agreed that somewhere around 70% to 85% should be appropriate, depending on personal financial circumstances (Aon Consulting and Georgia State University, 2008; Peng, 2008). This means that together, these three pillars should provide a replacement ratio up to that level. China's overall pension system falls short of this pension system model. It is currently dominated by the first pillar, which consists of three national public pension plans that cover most eligible adults in China. At the same time, the second pillar, which is employer-provided pension benefits, still only covers a small fraction of workers in urban areas outside the public sector, even though private-sector employers were allowed to set up enterprise annuities, as employer-provided pension plans are called in China, back in 2004. As for the third pillar, voluntary individual retirement accounts, they are almost nonexistent at this point. With such reliance on public pensions for the vast majority of the population, there will be concern about the long-term adequacy of pension benefits in retirement, in terms of supporting an adequate replacement ratio.

1.1.2 Coverage of the public pension plan

While the second and third pillars are important in terms of providing adequate financial security and an adequate replacement ratio, they tend to be voluntary, whereas the public pension plan is mandatory. Therefore, the focus of a national pension system is primarily on the first pillar, as it concerns almost everyone. The purpose of a public pension is that everyone in a country can be provided with some base level of financial security in retirement. This is especially the case in China, as the second pillar remains small and the third pillar is almost nonexistent. For the first pillar, one key issue is the coverage, meaning who is eligible for the public pension plan. Ideally, every country should have one national pension plan that covers every eligible adult, meaning there is one pension contribution rate and one pension formula that applies to everyone. In other words, everyone will be treated the same within one national plan. This is the case, for the most part, with the Social Security benefit of the United States.[1] However, in some other countries, it is not uncommon to have more than one public pension plan. The reasons for having multiple pension plans are mostly related to occupation, but they can also be related to geographic location. For example, Germany has different pension plans for farmers and miners, among other occupations, and Canada has a separate public pension plan for the province of Quebec (Chen and Turner, 2015). The biggest advantage of a uniform national plan is its transportability of pension benefits, regardless of what you do and where you live, as people can engage in several occupations and live in different places over their life. In this respect, China again shows some similarities with international practices but also some major differences.

China has three national public pension plans that cover most people in the country. However, that is where the similarity ends. What makes the Chinese public pension plans unique is their geographic fragmentation, which is exhibited in two ways:

- First, this fragmentation is based on where you live, whether in urban or rural areas, and what you do. Two national plans are for enterprise workers in urban areas and public sector employees, respectively, and the third plan is for everyone else, primarily targeting people working and living in rural areas, such as farmers, but also people living in urban areas with informal occupational opportunities. The reason for such a distinction between urban and rural areas is the household registration system in China, implemented soon after the founding of the People's Republic of China in 1949, to control population movement. The pension plans for urban workers, as they are mostly based on urban employer contributions, offer much higher pension benefits than those offered by the third national pension plan.
- Second, these three national plans are national in name only. Each one literally consists of 31 provincial-level public pension plans. Together, they

are considered a national plan, only in the sense that they follow the same general rules set by the central government in terms of pension contribution rate and benefits formula. Some of these provincial-level pension plan can even consist of multiple local city- or county-level pension plans. The major factors that separate one provincial or local plan from another are the basis for calculating employer pension contributions and pension benefits because they are both tied to local average wages. As the local average wage varies from one province to another, or from one city to another within a province, that can make the employer pension contribution and final pension benefit different for two workers even if they earn the same wage in two different provinces. Besides, these separate public pension plans are also administered at the provincial or local level, rather than at the central level. Such fragmentation will certainly lead to concerns over the fairness and portability of pension benefits, among other things.

1.1.3   *Financing of the public pension plan*

The third major aspect of a country's pension system is how the public pension is financed. There are two issues related to the financing mechanism. The first issue is whether the pension benefits are funded on a pay-as-you-go (PAYGO) basis or on an advance-funding basis. PAYGO means the current pension contributions from any source are used to pay for current retirees' pension benefits. PAYGO acts like an intergenerational revenue/cost transfer that provides social insurance, meaning that collectively, we ensure the financial security of current retirees. PAYGO, as expected, can lead to annual pension surpluses and deficits. The financial health of a pension plan funded on a PAYGO basis largely depends on the dependency ratio, the ratio of current workers paying into the plan over retirees receiving pension benefits from the plan. The higher the ratio, the better the financial health of the plan. This also means that the biggest threat to the long-term financial health of such a plan is a drop in this ratio, primarily as a result of the ageing of the population, holding all else constant. Advance funding means that through actuarial valuation, a worker's pension benefits are calculated and then funded over his or her working career so that the benefits will be fully funded by the time of retirement. Advance funding does not act as social insurance, but it is also not subject to the problem of population ageing.

By and large, public pension plans worldwide are funded on a PAYGO basis because as a society, we care more about the social insurance aspect of a public pension plan. Because of that, a public pension is subject to the negative effects of population ageing, which is happening in most industrialized countries. China is no exception in that respect. The pension plans for urban workers in both public and private sectors are funded on a PAYGO basis. Because of that, the long-term financial health of both plans is also negatively affected by the ageing of Chinese population. The difference, however, is that the ageing of Chinese population will happen at a much faster pace in the next several decades than that in most other major countries in the world, mostly as a result of its population control policy in the past.

The second financing issue with regard to a public pension plan is the source of funding. There are several related questions to this issue: whether there is a dedicated funding source for the public pension plan, whether this dedicated funding source is the only source of funding for the pension plan, and whether there is any general tax support for the public pension plan. Another way to think of this financing issue is whether the financing of public pension plans is completely separate from the rest of government finance, which relies mostly on general taxes. The international practice is to have one dedicated funding source, which is usually a tax on wages and salaries, shared by both employers and employees, and the public pension plan is supposed to be self-sufficient with this dedicated funding source, receiving no support from government's general taxes. That means that if there is a funding shortage, short-term or long-term, it has to be resolved within the pension plan itself, meaning either raising more revenue from the dedicated funding source or reducing pension benefits. The U.S. Social Security is a good example of that. Its primary source of funding is a payroll tax on wages and salaries, split between employers and employees. The only other source of revenue is interest income from the accumulation of past annual surpluses that have been invested in U.S. Treasury securities.

China's public pension plans share some similarities but also exhibit a major difference from this international practice. The pension plan for private-sector urban workers is primarily funded by employer and employee contributions based on their wages and salaries, with additional investment income from past surpluses. However, there is no clear line of separation between this dedicated source to finance the pension plan and the rest of government finance. Due to the size of legacy debt when the current pension plan was first established, the ageing of population, and the fragmentation of the pension plans at the local level, government general revenue transfer from all levels of government to subsidize some local pension plans facing annual funding deficits has been a norm and thus an integral part of pension financing in China, as can be seen in Table 2.6 in Chapter 2. There is also no clear government policy on the extent to which the public pension benefits should be subsidized by general taxes. As for the other national pension plan for urban and rural residents, it is designed so that a government general tax subsidy is an indispensable part of its financing, in addition to individual contributions. Therefore, it can be said that Chinese governments at all levels are the ultimate guarantors of public pension benefits. With the fast ageing of population in China, how much impact the financing of public pension benefits will have on government finance at all levels in the future deserves a lot of attention.

1.1.4 Summary

As can be seen in this brief comparison between China and international practices in three salient aspects of a national pension system, while China shares some similarities in all three aspects, it also exhibits some major differences. This brief comparison also provides a road map for this book in terms of its themes and focus. In this book, we explore these similarities more fully but more critically the differences, the reasons behind these differences, and what these differences mean for the sustainability and adequacy of China's pension system, especially the public pension plan part.

The rest of the book is structured as follows. In the remainder of this first chapter of the book, we provide a brief historical overview of how China's pension system has evolved into its current form since modern China was founded by the Chinese Communist Party in 1949. In the second chapter, we provide a detailed description of what the current pension system looks like, in terms of benefit design, funding, and governance. The third chapter is a complement to the second chapter, in that it provides detailed descriptions of public pension plans in three provinces as case studies to help us to gain a more in-depth understanding of the variations in public pensions across the country. These two chapters provide a context for the discussion in the fourth chapter, which is about the challenges facing the current pension system. The biggest challenge facing the pension system is the ageing of the Chinese population, which will lead to a significant long-term funding shortfall. This discussion naturally leads to the fifth chapter, which is about possible solutions to these challenges. The last chapter concludes.

One challenge in writing a book on the Chinese pension system is that the system is fairly new and continues to undergo frequent changes, as the central government continues to develop new policies to fine-tune various parts of the pension system, or even make major changes to the system, in response to long-term economic and demographic changes. As a result, some literature that was relevant in the past in addressing issues at the time may no longer be so at present, as the government has already made policy changes. Therefore, in writing this book, we rely primarily on official documents and statistics issued by the governments, mostly by the central government. We also rely on the latest reports published by the Chinese Academy of Social Sciences for actuarial valuations of Chinese public pension plans in 2019 and 2022. These reports are reviewed in Chapters 4 and 5.

1.2 A brief historical review

In this section, we provide a brief overview of the history of the Chinese pension system. Such a review informs us not only on how the current pension system came about but also on some of the historical issues that continue to challenge this pension system.

The history of the development of Chinese pension system into its current form can generally be divided into three periods: (1) pre-Cultural Revolution, the period between the founding of People's Republic of China and the Cultural Revolution (1949–1966), (2) the Cultural Revolution (1966–1976), and (3) post-Cultural Revolution (1976–present).

1.2.1 Pre-Cultural Revolution

Soon after the founding of the People's Republic of China in October 1949, the Chinese central government started drafting regulation for various insurance schemes for workers, modelled after the system established in the former Soviet Union. The first regulation was published and went into effect in 1951, called the "Labor Insurance Regulations of the People's Republic of China". It contained provisions for many aspects of labor insurance, including pensions. Even though this regulation has been revised multiple times since then, it contained some features of pension design that are still in force, and thus, a brief description of the parts concerning pensions is needed.

Article 15 of Chapter 2 of this regulation concerned remuneration during old age. A male (female) worker can receive a pension at the age of 60 (50) after working for 25 (20) years and at the current enterprise for at least five years (inclusive). The pension will be equal to 50% to 70% of his (her) final salary. The regulation applied to enterprises, state-run, public-private, and privately run, with more than 100 employees. In this regulation, there was a provision for collecting insurance premiums for all manners of insurance but not specifically for pensions. The total labor insurance premium amounted to 3% of an employee's salary and was entirely paid for by the employer and not deducted from the employee's salary. Thirty percent of the labor insurance funds paid each month would be deposited into the account of the All-China Federation of Trade Unions as general labor insurance funds, and the remaining 70% would be deposited into the account of the grassroots trade union of each enterprise as labor insurance funds. The insurance premiums were to be managed by the People's Bank of China, China's central bank.

This design had two important aspects. First, each enterprise was primarily responsible for its employees' pension, and second, the All-China Federation of Trade Unions at the national level collected a small portion of the premium to allocate nationwide as a secondary source of protection for workers across the country. While 3% of wages seemed somewhat low, the population at the time was young and the ratio of workers to retirees was also high. This system worked relatively smoothly till the Cultural Revolution in 1966.

In 1955, the State Council, China's highest-level governing agency, issued the "Temporary Measures on Managing the Retirement of Government Personnel". A male (female) employee, after 15 years of service, could retire at the age of 60 (55) and would receive a pension equal to 50% to 80% of final salary. There was no mention of any contribution that had to be made by the government employee and/or employer or who would pay the pension benefits. It was assumed that the pensions were to be fully paid out of state coffers.

These were the two major government regulations on public pensions early after the founding of modern China. One important observation on this early development is that from the very early stages, nationwide pension plans covered only two segments of the population. The first was employees working in enterprises in urban areas, whether state-run, privately run, or hybrid. The second was government employees, from central to local levels. Thus, from very early on, people living in rural areas were excluded from public pension plans, and people living in urban areas not employed by the government or enterprises were not covered by any pension plans either. These people were on their own or were supposed to be supported by their families in their old age. This feature of pension design largely endured till the end of the first decade of the 21st century.

So why did the government only concentrate on these two segments of the population to the exclusion of other parts of population? This can be understood from economic, administrative, and political perspectives. First, only workers in enterprises in urban areas and government employees drew a steady salary that made it possible to design a pension. Administratively, the government at the time most likely did not have the capacity to keep a record of the employment and wages of people living in rural areas. This was somewhat easier with workers in urban areas and government employees. To ensure the stability of the new government, it certainly needed to rely on the vast government bureaucracy, and therefore, it is no surprise that public-sector employees were provided with the best pension benefits. Second on the list were urban workers, as the new government would need them to modernize the country's dilapidated economy. This was also tied into China's economic development policy at the time. From the economic perspective, China wanted to develop a modern economy after its founding in 1949. Following the economic development model in the former Soviet Union, China chose to develop heavy industry first to catch up with the industrialized countries. Therefore, ensuring some basic security of livelihood in retirement was also one way to incentivize urban workers to put their best efforts into modernizing the economy. On the other side of this industrial policy, people living in the vast countryside paid the price. One way to amass the required capital for heavy industry was to squeeze the rural population, thus, the policy of "relying on the rural population to support the heavy industry" (Li, 2018).

To prevent the rural population from escaping this squeeze, soon after the founding of China, the new government established the household registration system, in which one is registered for permanent resident after birth at a location where one's parents are registered for permanent residence. Since all the social welfare programs, jobs, and education were tied to household registrations, this system essentially prevented people in rural areas from moving to urban areas, as they would not be able to find jobs and their children would not be able to go to local public schools. While the rigid household registration system has been loosened to some limited extent since the economic reform in the early eighties, it still remains mostly intact, as local governments in urban areas are resistant to major loosening of the system. They are protective of all the benefits, including pension benefits, given to their urban residents, and they do not want to dilute these benefits by sharing them with people coming from rural areas. This is also a major reason why China even now does not have a basic nationwide universal public pension plan.

1.2.2 Cultural Revolution

The ten-year Cultural Revolution that started in 1966, however, quickly wreaked havoc with the carefully laid out plan for urban workers. All institutions were damaged to some extent, including those managing pension benefits for urban workers. The All-China Union stopped its operation, thus severely affecting the collection of pension premiums from urban enterprises. As a result of this, the State Council in 1969 issued the "Opinions on Several Institutional Reforms in State Enterprises' Financial Works". It stipulated that enterprises were only responsible for the retirement benefits of their own employees, and they did not have to submit any premium to the national organization. Thus, the collection of labor insurance premiums was terminated in 1969. Some 400 million Chinese yuan (hereafter expressed in CNY) in the All-China Trade Union's pension reserve was even turned over to the national treasury to be used for any governmental purpose (Hu, 2003). Essentially, pensions for urban workers became the responsibility of each enterprise on a PAYGO basis, with no national backup funds to save for the future or help out with enterprises with weak finance. This way of funding urban workers' pensions continued until the first pension reform for urban workers in 1991. This is also the major reason for the legacy debt of current pension plans for urban workers. For workers during this period of time, nothing had been set aside for their future pension benefits.

1.2.3 Post-Cultural Revolution

The evolution of the Chinese pension system after the Cultural Revolution revolves around the establishment of public pension plans, almost in a chronological fashion, for three groups of people: urban enterprise workers, urban and rural residents, and public-sector employees.

1.2.3.1 Pension plan for urban enterprise workers

After the Cultural Revolution ended in 1976, China was in a recovery mode, even with regard to public pensions. In 1978, the State Council issued two directives with regard to pensions for the two groups of pensioners mentioned earlier: the "State Council's Temporary Measures on Workers' Retirement and Resignation" and the "State Council's Temporary Measures on Providing for Old, Weak, Sick, and Disabled Cadres". For workers, the retirement age stayed the same for both men (60) and women (50), with a minimum of ten years of service. The benefit level, however, became more generous. Depending on when a worker joined the workforce, which also determined the years of service, the benefit varied from 60% to 90% of final pay. The cost of pension payments was part of each enterprise's administrative expense. In other words, enterprises were still entirely responsible for their employees' pensions, with no government or individual contribution. As for government officials, the retirement age also remained the same for men (60) and women (55) but with a minimum of ten years of service. The benefit level was also the same as for enterprise workers, ranging from 60% to 90% of final pay, depending on the years of service. Compared to the rules established in the early fifties, one major difference between these two rules was that the benefit level was made more generous with fewer years of service, and it was uniform among enterprise workers and public-sector employees.

It turns out that the word "temporary", at least with regard to the regulation on enterprise workers, was a perfect fit. The year of 1978, in hindsight, was momentous in modern China because this was the year China embarked on a multi-decade journey of reforming its state-run economic model and opening up to the outside world. Prior to the reform, the economy was dominated by state-owned enterprises (SOEs) run by all levels of government with very little private-sector economy. In this planned economy, SOEs faced little market competition or risk of bankruptcy. A retired worker could count on his/her previous employer to provide pension benefits for him/her during retirement. All this changed with the "reform and opening" policy implemented in 1978. Privately run and foreign-owned companies were allowed. Market forces gradually replaced state planning to determine the productivity and profitability of a company. Market competition can force unprofitable companies to go bankrupt. During the reform, many SOEs went bankrupt or were acquired by private/foreign companies. The large-scale SOE layoffs also called for new programs to provide pension benefits for these laid-off workers when they reached retirement age. In addition, some old enterprises had much heavier burdens to support their retired workers/staff than newly established enterprises. Therefore, the old model of relying on your previous employer to provide all your pension benefits as a fixed percentage of final pay could no longer work, for the simple reason that some of these companies just disappeared.

The reform and open policy that started in 1978 inevitably forced policymakers to revise the pension financing model for urban workers. As with all kinds of reforms in China, given its size, the reform of pensions for urban workers started small as pilot programs in some urban areas so that the central government could learn about what worked and what did not work and then devise a nationwide policy. After years of experimentation, in 1991, the central government issued the "Decision on the Reform of the Enterprise Workers' Pension System". It required the establishment of basic pension plans, to which the enterprises should contribute and employees should contribute no more 3% of their wages. These pension plans were to be managed by municipal or county-level governments. However, the regulation left it to each municipality or county to decide how much each enterprise should contribute. The regulation also encouraged enterprises to establish supplemental pensions for their employees and for employees to establish individual retirement accounts. However, this regulation only applied to state-owned enterprises, but not to collectively, foreign-, or privately-owned companies. While the reform proposed in this regulation was very limited in its scope, the regulation was still significant in the sense that it established the concept that the financing of pensions should be the responsibility of three parties: the government (even though it was at the local level at this point), enterprises, and employees.

Due to the wide-ranging disparities allowed in this regulation among different regions, and after more years of experimentation, in 1997, the State Council issued the "Decision on Establishing a Unified Basic Pension System for Enterprise Workers". This regulation was a milestone in the history of reforming pension system in China, as it firmly established the concept of a basic pension plan for urban workers and how it was to be financed. The basic pension plan has two components, the base amount and another amount to be determined by individual accounts. The base amount is financed by a social pool of funds. Each employer contributes up to 20% of the employee's salary to the social pool, which is managed at the city/county government level. Each employee also contributes up to 8% of his/her salary to his/her individual account, with another 3% contributed by the enterprise. As for coverage, this regulation dictated that the basic pension plan should apply to employees in all kinds of enterprises, including state, collective, private, and foreign owned.

Finally, in 2005, the State Council issued the "Decision on Improving Enterprise Employees' Basic Pension System", also known as Document 38. It made changes to the decision issued in 1997 in a few areas and set new policy goals for the future:

- It reduced the contribution rate to the individual account from 11% to 8%, to be paid entirely by the worker, with no employer contribution to the individual account.
- It extended the coverage to include all self-employed workers.
- It called for a higher level of social pooling, meaning that pooling should take place at the provincial level, rather than at the city or county level.

- It brought in the concept of enterprise annuity as another component to the basic pension plan, although it is not required of every enterprise.

After years of experimentation, the contour of the basic pension plan for urban workers has finally come into focus as of this regulation: a base pension financed by mandatory contributions from urban enterprises into a social pool, a mandatory individual retirement account, and an optional enterprise annuity.

1.2.3.2 *Pension plans for urban and rural residents*

After more or less completing its work on basic pension plans for urban workers, the central government turned its attention to pensions for other segments of the population. One glaring omission from any nationwide pension system since the founding of China in 1949 was people living in rural areas, most of them farmers. Finally, the central government decided to do something about this. Traditionally, children (especially sons) and other family members were the major sources of old-age security for the elderly in rural areas. There were some limited old-age support programs in rural areas (such as the five guarantees program) funded by both rural collectives and township/county governments. While there had been some experiments with pension plans for people in rural areas since the 1980s, such plans primarily relied on personal savings and contributions with no social pooling or government subsidy. Thus, coverage was limited and the central government stopped its operation in the late nineties. In the early years of the 21st century, the central government started pilot plans in some areas, and in 2009, it issued the "Guidelines on Developing a New Rural Pension Insurance Pilot Project", signaling the start of modern pension plan for people living in rural areas that does not rely entirely on individual contributions. The new pension plan, like the one for urban enterprise workers, has two components: a base pension and an amount determined by an individual account. The base pension also has two parts: a minimum amount decided by the central government and an additional amount to be determined by the local government. This base pension is entirely paid by the central and local governments. For the individual account, the government sets several levels of individual contribution, and the local government is required to make some minimum contribution to individual accounts. One important difference between this plan and that for urban workers is that participation in this pension plan is voluntary for rural residents, whereas it is mandatory for urban workers to participate in their pension plan.

Then the central government turned its attention to another segment of the population that was excluded from previous pension plans. In 2011, the State Council issued the "State Council Guidelines on Developing an Urban Residents' Old-Age Social Insurance Pilot Project". It was applied to any residents living in urban areas who were not employed by a government entity or an urban enterprise and thus not covered by either a public pension for public-sector employees or a basic pension plan for urban enterprise workers. This pension plan looked almost exactly like that for rural residents mentioned earlier. The participation in this pension system was also voluntary for urban residents.

Because of the similarities between these two pension plans, the central government decided to merge them into one. In 2014, the State Council issued the "Opinion on Establishing a Unified Basic Old-Age Insurance System for Urban and Rural Residents". There were only minor changes in the terms of this unified pension plan from the two previous separate pension plans. While the 2009 regulation only established a rural pension plan on a pilot basis, this 2014 regulation essentially applied this basic pension plan to all residents in rural areas. Therefore, the establishment of this unified pension plan was a major milestone in the evolution of Chinese public pension plans.

1.2.3.3   Pension plan for public sector employees

With the establishment of this unified system for rural and urban residents, there remains one major issue to be resolved. It was the glaring difference in pension benefits between public-sector workers and urban enterprise workers in terms of benefit level and contribution, which the public considered unfair since public-sector workers would receive a more generous pension in retirement without having to making any contribution. As a result, in 2015, the State Council issued the "Decision on the Reform of the Pension System for Civil Servants and Employees of Public Institutions". It is essentially a replica of the pension plan for urban enterprise workers. The basic system also consists of three components: a social pooling contributed by government, an individual account contributed by employees, and an occupational annuity set up by individual government employers. The pension benefit level and contribution level are also the same as those for urban enterprise employees. The setup of the occupational annuity, however, is mandatory for public sector employers.

This regulation completes the most important part of the reform effort to establish a modern pension system in China that incorporates the first two pillars of an ideal three-pillar pension system. The first pillar consists of three public pension plans, one for public sector workers, one for urban enterprise workers, and another for everyone else, primarily people living in rural areas. China can finally claim that it now has a network of three public pension plans that theoretically can cover everyone in the country. For all three plans, there are two essential components: a base pension paid by employers or governments at all levels and an individual account. In principle, this is more in line with the modern design of public pension plans in other countries, which rely on both employer/government contributions and individual contributions. The second pillar consists of a voluntary enterprise annuity for urban enterprise workers and a mandatory occupational annuity for public-sector workers. Through multiple rounds of reform, the current pension system in China has come a long way from the initial pension design in the early 1950s, when basically every enterprise was only responsible for its own workers' pension benefits.

In the next chapter, we discuss in detail how these three pension plans are designed and governed, in terms of pension benefit level and pension contribution level, for both the base pension and the individual account, plus other governance issues to address the funding shortage in basic pension plans.

Note

1 Some state and local government employees, for historical reasons, are exempt from the Social Security system because these states had already established their own pensions before the Social Security system was established.

References

Aon Consulting and Georgia State University. 2008. Replacement Ratio Study: A Measurement Tool for Retirement Planning. Chicago, IL: Aon Consulting.

Chen, Tianhong, and John A. Turner. 2015. Fragmentation in Social Security Old-Age Benefit Provision in China. *Journal of Aging & Social Policy*, 27: 107–122.

Hu, Xiaoyi. 2003. Historical Evolution of Chinese Old-Age Insurance System. *Jing Ji Yao Can*, 15: 26–32. (in Chinese)

Li, Mengyao. 2018. Public Pension System in Transition Economy: Analysis on China's Historical Pension Reform Under Economic and Demographic Change. *Management Science and Engineering*, 12(3): 30–50.

Peng, Jun. 2008. State and Local Pension Fund Management. Boca Raton, FL: CRC Press.

World Bank. 1994. Averting the Old Age Crisis: Policies to Protect the Old and Promote Growth. Oxford University Press. Available at https://documents1.worldbank.org/curated/en/973571468174557899/pdf/multi-page.pdf.

World Bank. 2022. Gross Domestic Product 2021. Available at https://databankfiles.worldbank.org/data/download/GDP. pdf.

2 Benefit design and governance

In this chapter, we first discuss how the three pension plans, mentioned in the first chapter, are designed. Then we discuss the scope of these pension plans, in terms of enrollment and financial data. After that, we address the governance of these pension plans. Finally, we look at the role the central government plays in the financing of public pension plans, in the context of the National Social Security Fund, the central adjustment fund mechanism, and the most recent development of national coordination of pension plans for urban enterprise workers.

2.1 Pension plan design

In this section, we describe how the three pension plans are designed.

2.1.1 Basic pension plan for urban enterprise workers

The benefits for urban employees have two major components: mandatory basic pension benefits and a voluntary enterprise annuity, laid out in State Council Document 38 issued in 2005, as mentioned in the previous chapter.

2.1.1.1 Basic pension benefits

The basic pension benefits for urban workers consist of two separate components, funded from two different sources, with the base amount from the social pool and another amount determined by the balance in individual accounts.

A. SOCIAL POOL

The mandatory social pool is entirely funded by employers of urban workers. Until 2019, contributions equal to 20% of the employees' wages were paid by employers into the social pool. This contribution rate, however, was reduced to 16% as of May 1, 2019, without a reduction in pension benefits,

DOI: 10.4324/9781003091974-2

as part of central government's policy to reduce the burden on enterprises, according to the regulation issued by the State Council in April 2019, titled the "Comprehensive Plan on Reducing Social Insurance Contribution Rates". Another stipulation for the employer contribution is that the total annual contribution cannot be more than 300% or less than 60% of the average local wages, meaning that workers earning more than 300% or less than 60% of the average local wage are treated as if they earn exactly at those two levels. This social pooling plan is funded on a PAYGO basis. Due to its pooling nature, the important question is at what level of government the funds are pooled. Since its inception, the pooling has been primarily done at the municipal or county level, and thus, the average local wage then refers to the average within a city or county, rather than a provincial or national average wage. As of the end of 2021, however, the central government required all provinces to pool at the provincial level, rather than at the city or county level.

To receive the base pension benefit from the social pool, a worker has to work for at least 15 years and retire at the age of 60 for men and 50 for blue-collar women (55 for white-collar women). The pension benefit is calculated as follows: it is equal to 1% of the mean of the average local wage of last year and the average of the worker's indexed wages over the period of contribution, for each year of service. This means that after a minimum of 15 years of contribution, the base pension amount guarantees a minimum replacement ratio of 15% of salary prior to retirement. If a worker works for less than 15 years, and thus, the employer contributes less than 15 years into the social pool, then the worker will not receive any base pension benefit from the social pool after retirement.

Two aspects of the pension benefit determination are worth further discussion. First, since it is a mean of the local average wage and the worker's own historical wages, then if the worker's average historical wage is lower (higher) than the current local average wage, he will get a higher (lower) pension than one simply based on his own wages over time. A pension benefit designed this way thus serves two purposes. It serves not just the purpose of insurance for financial security in retirement but also the purpose of redistribution, or social welfare. In this case, the higher-wage workers are subsidizing part of lower-wage workers' pensions in a particular local area. Second, because a significant part of the pension benefit is tied to local wages, it creates disparities in basic pension amounts across the country, as a result of uneven economic development among different regions of the country, leading to large disparities in local wages. The reason the benefit is tied to local wages, either at the city or provincial level, is that, as discussed earlier, when the public pension plan was first designed, it was mostly administered at the local level. Since each city or county collects and pools the contributions and distributes the benefits to retirees within its local jurisdiction, it makes sense that the benefit will be based on local wages. This disparity also applies to employer

Table 2.1 Annual Pension Benefit Growth Rate

Year	Growth Rate	Year	Growth Rate
2006	23.7%	2015	10.0%
2007	9.1%	2016	6.5%
2008	10.0%	2017	5.5%
2009	10.0%	2018	5.0%
2010	10.0%	2019	5.0%
2011	10.0%	2020	5.0%
2012	10.0%	2021	4.5%
2013	10.0%	2022	4.0%
2014	10.0%		

Source: MOHRSS and MOF announcements, various years.

contributions, as the contribution is within a band of 60% to 300% of local average wages. Thus, employers in high-income areas will contribute more to social pools than those in low-income areas. While this is not a problem when the social pooling is administered at the local level, it will become a problem when it is done at a provincial or national level due to the disparity between provincial/national average wages and local average wages.

While the base pension in the first year of retirement is determined by this formula, the increase in the base pension in the years after retirement is determined by the central government. Every year, the Ministry of Human Resources and Social Security (MOHRSS) and the Ministry of Finance (MOF) jointly issue a notice about the rate of increase for the basic pension benefit. The rate of increase is loosely based on the average salary growth rate and inflation rate. Table 2.1 shows the annual pension growth rate between 2006, the year when the central government decided to standardize the growth rate across the country, and 2021.[1] As can be seen, until 2015, the rate was about 10%. Since then, the rate has been on a fairly consistent downward trend, ending at 4% in 2021. Any increase in pension benefit is paid out of the social pool.

B. MANDATORY INDIVIDUAL ACCOUNT

The second part of the pension benefit is funded by the individual account that is financed with contributions of 8% of wages from the individual worker (Document 38). After 15 years of contribution into the individual account, the retiree is eligible to receive benefits based on the balance of the individual account upon retirement. The monthly benefit amount is equal to the account balance divided by a factor, which is based on the retirement age, life expectancy, and interest rate. For example, at the retirement age of 60 for men, this factor is 139, meaning the account will be depleted in 139 months, or 11.5 years. In other words, the balance will be exhausted when the man reaches 71.5 years old. For woman retiring at the age of 50, the factor is 195. The earlier/later you retire, the greater/smaller the factor is, meaning it takes more/fewer months to draw down the balance, and thus, a smaller/ larger monthly payment. Table 2.2 shows the factors related to various retirement ages.

If a worker contributes less than 15 years to his/her individual account and then retires, the retiree does not qualify for the basic pension and will receive his/her individual account balance in one lump sum. If a man retires at the age of 60 after contributing more than 15 years, and dies before the age of 71.5, then the remaining balance in his individual account can be inherited by his surviving relatives. However, if he lives past the age of 71.5 and exhausts the funds in his individual account, this payment will still continue till his death. Since his individual account is exhausted, this payment now will be paid out of the social pool. This is the same for a woman. If she retires at the age of 50 and lives beyond age 66 (adding 195 months), she will continue to be paid the same amount as before her individual account is exhausted.

The balance of individual accounts grows at a rate set by the government. Until 2016, this rate was tied to the short-term, such as one-year, rate on bank deposits. Because this is a short-term rate, it is typically very low, leading to very slow growth of the individual account's value. Since each province could set its own rate, the rate varied from province to province. Because of such disparities across the country, in 2017, the MOHRSS and the MOF issued a notice, titled "Unify and Standardize the Method for Bookkeeping

Table 2.2 Retirement Age and Related Withdrawal Factor

Age	Factor	Age	Factor
40	233	56	164
41	230	57	158
42	226	58	152
43	223	59	145
44	220	60	139
45	216	61	132
46	212	62	125
47	208	63	117
48	204	64	109
49	199	65	101
50	195	66	93
51	190	67	84
52	185	68	75
53	180	69	65
54	175	70	56
55	170		

Source: Chinese State Council, Document 38 issued in 2005. Available at www.gov.cn/zhengce/content/2008-03/28/content_7376.htm.

Interest Rate of Individual Accounts of Workers' Pension". It stated that the rate will be set by the central government every year. The rate applied for 2016 was 8.31%. This rate was set at 7.12%, 8.29%, 7.61%, 6.04%, 6.69%, and 6.12% respectively for 2017 through 2022. These rates were substantially higher than the short-term bank deposit rates, leading to a much faster growth of individual account balances.

C. REPLACEMENT RATIO

In explaining the "Decision on Improving Enterprise Employees' Basic Pension System" issued by the State Council in 2005, the MOHRSS stated that the policy goal of this pension design, combining social pooling and individual accounts, was to generate a pension replacement ratio of 59.2%: 35% from the social pooling (assuming 35 years of working, and according to the formula, each year of working replaces 1% of pre-retirement wages) and 24.2% from the individual retirement account.[2]

It should also be recognized that this replacement ratio of 59.2% was based on the original employer contribution rate of 20%. Since this contribution rate was reduced to 16% in 2019, then it should be assumed that this replacement ratio of 59% can only be achieved after 2019 at the expense of quickly draining the balance in the social pool, or the replacement ratio will need to be reduced.

2.1.1.2   Enterprise annuity

The second component of pension benefits for urban workers is known as the "enterprise annuity". It is a voluntary, fully funded defined contribution pension plan, as a supplemental pension plan for urban enterprise workers. In 2004, the MOHRSS issued the "Provisional Measures on Enterprise Annuity", allowing for the establishment of enterprise annuities. At the time, it was financed either exclusively by employer contributions or by a mix of employer and employee contributions, up to a (combined) maximum of 1/12 (or about 8%) of the annual salary. The contribution would go to an employee's individual account. This notice was eventually replaced by the "Measures on Enterprise Annuity" issued by the MOHRSS in 2016 that went into effect in February 2018. This rule sets the contribution rate as follows: the employer can contribute up to 8% of the company's total payroll; and the total contribution, including both employer and employee contributions, cannot exceed 12% of the company's total payroll. This is a higher level of contribution than that in the previous rule. It also means that the company's contribution to each individual employee does not have to be based on the same percentage of salary, with higher percentages as rewards for better performance. As the difference in percentages can lead to wide disparity in the total company contribution amount among employees, the measures also stipulate that the highest company contribution amount cannot be more than five times the average company contribution amount. Employee contribution will always go to the employee's individual account. The measures leave it to each company to decide the vesting period for the company's contribution. The vesting period can be zero, meaning the employees own 100% of the company's contribution from Day 1, or the company can decide that the employee will own a growing proportion of company's contribution with each year of service. However, the measures also stipulate that the vesting period cannot exceed eight years, meaning that after eight years of service, the employee owns 100% of the company's contributions plus investment return on the contributions.

2.1.2   *Pension plan for public sector employees*

This pension plan covers employees of government agencies of all levels and public institutions, such as public universities and hospitals. After the pension reform for public-sector employees beginning in 2015, the overall design of their pension benefits conforms to that for urban enterprise workers.

2.1.2.1   *Basic pension benefits*

The basic pension benefits are designed exactly like those for urban enterprise workers, consisting of two parts, one funded by social pooling and the other funded by individual accounts. Because the basic benefits are exactly the same for these two plans, please refer to Section 2.1.1.1 for a detailed description of the design of basic pension benefits.

2.1.2.2   *Occupational annuity*

The pension reform also requires public sector employers to set up an occupational annuity, similar to the enterprise annuity, as a supplement to the basic pension benefit. Every year, the government employer will contribute 8% of the employee's salary to his/her individual account, and the employee will contribute 4% of his/her salary to the individual account. The overall contribution rate is the same as the maximum contribution rate for enterprise annuity. While occupational annuity is structured similarly to enterprise annuity, there is one big difference: the setup of an enterprise annuity is optional for an enterprise, whereas an occupational annuity is mandatory for public-sector employers. The reason for this is to reduce public-sector employees' resistance to pension reform. Prior to pension reform, the replacement ratio of public pension was in the 70% to 100% range. With the pension reform, the basic pension benefit's replacement ratio was not nearly as high. With the mandatory occupational annuity, the replacement ratio will remain similar to that prior to the pension reform.

In 2015, the State Council issued a directive called the "State Agency and Public Institution Occupational Annuity Method" to explain further how to set up the annuity. While the employer's 8% contribution is credited to the individual employee, it is notional only and it grows at an interest rate set by the state each year. The employee's 4% contribution is directly deposited into the individual account and is invested by an investment firm selected by the government. The actual investment return will determine how fast the account balance grows, according to the "Unify and Standardize the Method for Book-keeping Interest Rate of Individual Accounts of Workers' Pension" regulation issued by the MOHRSS in 2017 mentioned earlier.

2.1.3   *Unified rural and urban residents' pension plan*

This plan covers anyone over 16 who is not a student in school and not covered by the two pension plans mentioned earlier. One fundamental difference between this plan and the other two plans is that participation in this plan is entirely voluntary, whereas participation in the other two plans is mandatory. Financial subsidy is the primary incentive for the government to encourage participation in this plan. The pension benefit also consists of two parts: base pension and individual account.

A) Base pension: the base pension is entirely funded by government tax revenues at all levels. The minimum level of base pension is set by the central government, and it is adjusted upward according to economic development and commodity prices. For example, in 2012, the base pension was CYN55 per month, and it was increased to CNY 70 in 2015, then to CYN88 in 2018,[3] and then again increased to CNY 93 in 2020.[4] The central government pays for 100% of the base pension for provinces in the mid and western (poorer) part of the country and 50% of the base pension for provinces in the eastern part of the country. Provincial and local governments can increase the minimum benefit level set by the central government with their own funds. Because of this, this total base amount varies significantly from one province to another. For example, in 2019, the base amount in Shanghai, one of the richest provincial-level municipalities in China, was CNY 1,010, whereas it was only CNY 103 in Henan province, one of the poorest provinces in China.[5] However, to receive this base pension benefit, the beneficiary also has to contribute to an individual account for at least 15 years, which determines the second part of pension benefit. This is one way by the government to encourage people to contribute to individual account and thus increase their pension benefit so that they can collect this base pension.

B) Individual account: The second part of the pension benefit comes from the individual account. There are two sources of funding for this account. The first funding source is individual contributions. While the central government has suggested many different levels of annual contribution, it is up to the individual provinces to set up their own contribution levels, and they can make changes to contribution levels in the future. Each individual contribution level corresponds to a certain payment schedule. The higher the contribution, the higher the nominal pension payment from the individual account in the future. The second funding source is government subsidy to individual accounts, with the amount of subsidy based on the level of individual contribution. The higher the individual contribution amount, the greater the government subsidy is. This subsidy is the second way by the government to encourage people not only to contribute but also to contribute at a higher level to their individual accounts. Just like the individual contribution amount, it is also up to the individual provinces to determine what the subsidy amount is for each contribution level. Due to the provincial discretion over contribution levels and government subsidy amounts, significant variation among provinces should be expected. Table 2.3 gives an example of such a variation between Shanghai and Jiangxi. While the levels of contribution are not significantly different between the two areas, the Shanghai government provides a more generous subsidy than the Jiangxi government does. When a beneficiary turns 60 after paying into

Table 2.3 Annual Individual Account Contribution Levels and Government Subsidies (in CNY)

Shanghai		Jiangxi	
Individual Contribution	Government Subsidy	Individual Contribution	Government Subsidy
500	200	300	40
700	250	400	50
900	300	500	60
1,100	350	600	65
1,300	400	700	70
1,700	450	800	75
2,300	525	900	80
3,300	575	1,000	85
4,300	625	1,500	90
5,300	675	2,000	95
		3,000	100
		4,000	150
		5,000	190
		6,000	230

Sources: Shanghai: Shanghai Municipal Urban and Rural Residents' Basic Pension Insurance Methods, effective May 1, 2019, available at http://sh.sina.com.cn/news/m/2019-04-25/detail-ihvhiewr8223961.shtml; Jiangxi: Jiangxi Provincial HRSS Department: Notice on Adjusting Provincial Urban and Rural Residents' Basic Pension Contribution Rate and Subsidy, issued in 2022, available at http://rst.jiangxi.gov.cn/art/2022/5/9/art_47858_3954259.html.

the account for at least 15 years, he/she starts to receive a monthly benefit from the individual account for a maximum 139 months. Accumulated individual funds are inheritable, except for the government subsidy.

C) Unique nature of benefits: the nature of benefits in this plan is fundamentally different from that of the other two plans. While the pension benefits of the other two plans are based on employment and wages earned, contributed by both employers and employees, the benefits of this plan are completely detached from employment. While individuals need to make contributions at a level of their own choosing, the overall benefit is heavily subsidized by governments at all levels, including the base pension and the matching fund for individual contributions. The base pension does not change with a given level of individual contribution or how many years you contribute to your individual account, after a minimum of 15 years. While the government encourages individuals to plan for retirement through individual accounts, the main draw of this pension plan for any participant is the base amount that is paid by the government. As the base amount is relatively small, the base pension plus any distribution from the individual account (especially if someone contributes at the lower level to draw down the base pension) will not be sufficient to maintain an adequate quality of life in most, if not all areas of China. Therefore, this pension plan acts more like a social welfare program than a traditional pension program. While it cannot provide an adequate pension, it strives to provide some bare minimum level of financial support in retirement so that retired people will not be completely destitute. Because of the joint financial support from all levels of government, the financial burden thus is not too onerous on any level of government, allowing the plan to reach a broad swath of population at a relatively low cost. Because the base amount is not automatically indexed to inflation and the government has discretion over how often and how much to increase it, the overall cost of the plan is more controllable from the government's perspective, making this plan a unique Chinese policy invention. Because of all these differences, this pension plan is not comparable to the other two pension plans. Therefore, in our discussion about the challenges facing Chinese pension system and the solutions in Chapters 4 and 5, the focus is primarily on the other two pension plans.

2.1.4 *Summary*

Table 2.4 provides a summary comparison of the basic features of the three pension plans in China. One feature of the overall pension system stands out. Even with all the reforms, it still remains a somewhat inequitable system in terms of benefit level. First, the benefit level of the plan for urban and rural residents is far below that of the other two plans. Second, the benefits for public-sector employees as a group still remain more generous than those for urban enterprise workers because the occupational annuity is mandatory, whereas the enterprise annuity is voluntary, and as discussed in the next section, it is

Table 2.4 Comparison of the Three Public Pension Plans

Pension Plan	Contribution	Basic Pension Benefits	Eligibility for Pension Benefits	Supplementary Benefits
Urban enterprise workers	Social pool: employer contributes 16% of salary; Individual account: employee contributes 8%	Social pool: 1%* (mean local wage + indexed worker wage) for each year of contribution; Individual account: 1/139th of account balance for 139 months	Needs to contribute to the social pool and individual accounts for at least 15 years; Man: 60 Woman: 50/55	Voluntary enterprise annuity: Employer: up to 8% of salary; Employee: up to 4%
Public sector employees	Social pool: employer contributes 16% of salary; Individual account: employee contributes 8%	Social pool: 1%* (mean local wage + indexed worker wages) for each year of contribution; Individual account: 1/139th of account balance for 139 months	Needs to contribute to the social pool and individual accounts for at least 15 years; Man: 60 Woman: 50/55	Mandatory occupational annuity: Employer: 8% of salary; Employee: 4% of salary
Urban and rural residents	Individual account: can contribute at different levels set up by each provincial government, with higher contribution amounts matched by a larger government subsidy.	Base pension: the central government sets the minimum base monthly amount nationwide, CNY 93 as of 2022, but each provincial government can set a higher base amount; this base amount is entirely paid by the government. Individual account: 1/139th of the balance every month for 139 months.	Needs to be 60 and contribute into an individual account for at least 15 years to receive the base pension plus the pension payments from individual accounts.	

not widely available. Even though a civil servant has to contribute 4% of his/ her own salary to an occupational annuity, the employer's contribution of 8% every year over a career, plus interest, makes a significant difference at the end in terms of pension benefit level. What also matters is that since these are government employers, the 8% contribution to occupational annuity is essentially a government subsidy to civil servants' pension benefits coming out of the government budget. Viewed from this perspective, then, civil servants are still favored over urban workers. Such equity issues, however, exist in other countries as well. For example, in the United States, state and local government employees' occupational pension benefits, on average, are more generous than those for workers in the private sector. The major difference is that the federal government does not tell employers what kind of pension benefits they should provide to their employees. It is entirely up to each employer, private or public, to determine the level of occupational pension benefit. In addition, the employer-provided pension benefit varies significantly from one employer to another, even within the public sector.

2.2 Scope of the three pension plans: Enrollment and financing

With this understanding of the design of these three basic plans, we can describe the scope of these three plans, primarily in terms of total coverage and financing, and the historical trends of such data. Unless otherwise noticed, the data come from the annual bulletins of MOHRSS.[6]

2.2.1 *Pension plan for urban enterprise workers*

Table 2.5 presents the historical data on the enrollment in this pension plan and the dependency ratio, or the ratio of current workers over retirees. One major turning point in this trend of enrollment for this pension plan happened in 2015, when the pension plan for public sector employees was reformed and it conformed to the plan for urban enterprise workers, as explained earlier. As a result, the data for these two plans were merged by MOHRSS for reporting purposes beginning in 2015, not only for enrollment but also for other financial data. For example, the total number of plan participants in 2017 included 37 million public sector employees (Fang and Feng, 2018).[7]

In 2021, 481 million urban enterprise workers, public-sector employees, and retirees were covered by this pension plan. Since the beginning of this century, the coverage has increased by about 240%, a reflection of not only a bigger workforce and inclusion of public-sector employees since 2015 but also an increase in the percentage of the workforce being covered. A more concerning number, however, is the dependency ratio. Until 2011, when this

Table 2.5 Number of Participants in Basic Pension Plans for Urban Enterprise Workers and Public-Sector Employees Who were Included after 2015 (in millions)

Year	Total Participants	Workers	Retirees	Dependency Ratio
2001	141.8	108.0	33.8	3.19
2002	147.4	111.3	36.1	3.08
2003	155.1	116.5	38.6	3.02
2004	163.5	122.5	41.0	2.99
2005	174.9	131.2	43.7	3.00
2006	187.7	141.3	46.4	3.05
2007	201.4	151.8	49.5	3.06
2008	218.9	165.9	53.0	3.13
2009	235.5	177.4	58.1	3.06
2010	257.1	194.0	63.1	3.08
2011	283.9	215.7	68.3	3.16
2012	304.3	229.8	74.5	3.09
2013	322.2	241.8	80.4	3.01
2014	341.2	255.3	85.9	2.97
2015	353.6	262.2	91.4	2.87
2016	379.3	278.3	101.0	2.75
2017	402.9	292.7	110.3	2.65
2018	419.0	301.0	118.0	2.55
2019	434.9	311.8	123.1	2.53
2020	456.2	328.6	127.6	2.57
2021	480.7	349.2	131.6	2.65

Source: MOHRSS annual bulletins, various years.

ratio reached a high of 3.16, meaning 3.16 workers supporting one retiree, it remained relatively steady around three. Since then, it has been on a gradual downward trend, and it reached 2.65 in 2021. (As will be explained in Chapter 4, the actual dependency ratio is even lower than this.) This certainly has serious implications for the sustainability of pension plan, a topic Chapter 4 explores further.

Another concerning number is the pension coverage among all eligible workers in urban areas. According to the 2021 annual bulletin issued by MOHRSS, there were 467.7 million workers in urban areas. With 349.2 million of them covered by basic pension plans in 2021, that means that about 25% of eligible workers were not covered by the basic pension plan. While this was an improvement from a coverage ratio of 60% over a ten-year period since 2011, it still means that a fairly high percentage of eligible workers is still not covered.

Table 2.6 presents historical data on the financing of this pension plan.

In 2021, the overall revenue collected by this pension plan (including revenue from the smaller plan for public-sector employees) stood at CNY 6.05 trillion. However, this amount has experienced a lot of volatility in recent

Table 2.6 Basic Pension Plan Financial Data (in billions)

Year	Total Revenue	Contribution	Government Subsidy	Expenditure	Cumulative Balance
2001	249			232	105
2002	317	255	41	284	161
2003	368	304	53	312	221
2004	426	359	61	350	298
2005	509	431	65	404	404
2006	631	522	97	490	549
2007	783	649	116	597	739
2008	974	802	144	739	993
2009	1,149	953	165	889	1,253
2010	1,342	1,111	195	1,056	1,537
2011	1,690	1,396	227	1,277	1,950
2012	2,000	1,647	265	1,556	2,394
2013	2,268	1,863	302	1,847	2,827
2014	2,531	2,043	355	2,176	3,180
2015	2,934	2,302	472	2,581	3,535
2016	3,506	2,677	651	3,185	3,858
2017	4,331	3,340	800	3,805	4,389
2018	5,117			4,465	5,090
2019	5,292			4,923	5,462
2020	4,438			5,130	4,832
2021	6,046			5,648	5,257

Source: MOHRSS annual bulletins, various years.

years. It decreased by about CNY 800 billion from 2019 to 2020, a reflection of the decrease in employer contribution rate from 20% to 16% for the whole year in 2020 and economic dislocation due to the COVID-19 outbreak. Then in 2021, it increased by CNY 1.6 trillion. The revenue stream consists of three parts, the revenue collected from contributions made by paying employers (into social pooling) and paying workers (into individual accounts), investment income on the cumulative balance, and government subsidies. The worrying trend is that government subsidies, while remaining relatively steady as a percentage of total revenue and reaching a low of 13% in 2013, have been accounting for an increasing percentage of total revenue in recent years, reaching a high of 18.5% in 2017.[8] As a matter of fact, the total expenditure has exceeded the contributions collected from employers and employees since 2014. This is partly connected to the declining ratio of paying workers to retirees discussed earlier. However, due to government subsidies, the plan's total revenue still exceeded total expenditure, except for 2020, and thus allowed the cumulative balance of the plan to continue to grow, reaching a peak of CNY 5.46 trillion in 2019. The balance declined in 2020, due to the reduction in employer contribution rate, although it bounced back somewhat to end at CNY 5.25 trillion in 2021.

In addition to the basic plan, there is also the enterprise annuity as a supplement to urban workers. Table 2.7 provides data on the participation in and asset values of enterprise annuities.

As of 2021, enterprise annuity was available to about 29 million urban workers from 117,500 enterprises, a small fraction of the urban enterprise workers covered by the basic plan, and that ratio has remained fairly static since 2012. Years after its implementation, the enterprise annuity has not become an important part of pension benefits for the overwhelming majority of workers in the basic plan, showing the limited appeal of enterprise annuities to either employers or employees. The total assets invested were valued at CNY 2.61 trillion in 2021.

2.2.2 *Pension plan for urban and rural residents*

Table 2.8 presents data on the enrollment in and financing of this plan.

As of 2021, 548 million people were covered by this plan, and of these, 162 million, or about 30%, were collecting pensions. This number increased substantially between 2009 and 2012, with the establishment of the pension plan for rural residents in 2009 and then the pension plan for urban residents, although the two plans were merged in 2014. Since 2012, the enrollment has increased more slowly. Between 2012 and 2021, the overall enrollment increased by only 13%. As comparison, over the same period, the enrollment in the pension plan for urban workers and public sector employees increased

Table 2.7 Historical Data on Participation in and Asset Values of Enterprise Annuities

Year	Participating Enterprises (in Thousands)	Participating Workers (in Millions)	Fund Balance (in Billions)
2006	24.0	9.6	91
2007	32.0	9.3	152
2008	33.0	10.4	191
2009	33.5	1.2	253
2010	37.1	13.4	281
2011	44.9	26.9	357
2012	54.7	18.5	482
2013	66.1	20.6	604
2014	73.3	22.9	769
2015	75.5	23.2	953
2016	76.3	23.3	1,108
2017	80.4	23.3	1,288
2018	87.4	23.9	1,477
2019	96.0	25.5	1,799
2020	105.0	27.2	2,250
2021	117.5	28.8	2,610

Source: MOHRSS annual bulletins, various years.

Table 2.8 Participants and Finance of Pension Plan for Urban and Rural Residents

Year	Total Participants (Millions)	Benefit Recipients (Millions)	Total Revenue (Billions)	Individual Contribution (Billions)	Expenditure (Billions)	Cumulative Balance (Billions)
2010	102.8	28.6	45.3	22.5	20.0	42.3
2011	331.8	8.8	111.0	42.1	59.9	123.1
2012	483.7	130.8	182.9	59.4	115.0	230.2
2013	497.5	137.7	205.2	63.6	134.8	300.6
2014	501.1	143.1	231.0	66.6	157.1	384.5
2015	504.7	148.0	285.5	70.0	211.7	459.2
2016	508.5	152.7	239.9	73.2	215.0	538.5
2017	512.6	156.0	330.4	81.0	237.2	631.8
2018	523.9	159.0	383.8		290.6	725.0
2019	532.7	160.3	410.7		311.4	824.9
2020	542.4	160.7	485.3		335.5	975.9
2021	548.0	162.1	533.9		371.5	1,139.6

Source: MOHRSS annual bulletins, various years.

by 58%. Total revenue in 2021 was CNY 534 billion. While the government only reported individual contributions as one source of revenue, which was CNY 81 billion in 2017 (the reporting on this number was discontinued after 2017), the difference between that and the total revenue in that year should be assumed to be mostly government subsidies plus some investment income on the cumulative balance. The total expenditure of CNY 237 billion in 2017 was also mostly paid by government subsidies. It should also be noted that of the annual total revenue, individual contribution has been accounting for a gradually decreasing percentage in recent years, indicating that government subsidy has been increasing in both absolute terms and percentage wise. The total cumulative balance of this plan stood at CNY 1.14 trillion in 2021. Since there is no social pooling in this plan, all this balance should belong to individual accounts. If we divide the fund balance by the number of total participants, we arrive at an average fund balance of about CNY 2,000 for each participant, a relatively small amount. This is also confirmed by the average annual contribution. If we divide the individual contribution amount in 2017 by the paying participants in that year (total participants minus benefit recipients), then the average contribution was CNY 227 per paying participant. It was even smaller at CNY 177 in 2013. This is an indication that a very significant number of the participants contribute a very small amount into their individual accounts to receive the base pension amount promised by the government. This also means that many of them do not see this plan as a means to save for retirement, but rather, they treat it more like a welfare program.

This view of the pension benefit is also reflected in the benefit level for pensioners of this plan, as it is much lower than that of the plan for urban workers. If we simply divide the total expenditure by the number of pensioners, we find that in 2021, the average benefit level for pensioners in the pension plan for urban and rural residents was CNY 2,291, whereas that for the pensioners in the plan for urban workers was CNY 42,928, or about 20 times larger.[9] Even though these are just average numbers and thus mask significant variations among different regions, they still give us some indication of the disparity in pension benefit levels between these two plans.

2.2.3   *Pension plan for public-sector employees*

As mentioned earlier, in 2015, the pension plan for public-sector employees was reformed and merged with the plan for urban enterprise workers, at least for reporting purposes, with no separate reporting for its enrollment and financing. The only data available for this plan reported separately by the MOHRSS is the value of occupational annuity, starting in 2020. The value of occupational annuity stood at CNY 1.79 trillion in 2021, an increase of CNY 500 billion over 2020. For comparison, the enterprise annuity increased by CNY 350 billion from 2020 to 2021, despite a larger base. Compared to the total value of CNY 2.61 trillion in enterprise annuity, after being in existence for a much longer period of time, it is possible that the occupational annuity will be larger than enterprise annuity in the near future, primarily due to its mandatory nature.

2.2.4   *Summary*

As of 2021, these three pension plans covered a total of 1.029 billion people, or about 73% of the population. When excluding those under 16 years and those in school over that age (totaling about 0.3 billion), the coverage ratio should be even higher. From this ratio alone, we can say that China has made significant progress in achieving its goal of making public pensions available to most citizens in the country in a relatively short period of time.

2.3   Governance

Governance centers on the social pool and individual pension plan accounts for urban enterprise workers, enterprise annuities, individual accounts and occupational annuities of pension plans for public sector employees, and individual accounts for urban and rural residents' pension plans.

2.3.1   *Pension plans for urban enterprise workers*

The social pool and individual accounts of this plan have traditionally been administered by local governments, up to the provincial level in some provinces, in the sense that these local governments collect contributions from enterprise employers and workers, make payments to retirees, and manage the cumulative balance, if there is one, within their jurisdictions. There has been a major effort by the central government in recent years to encourage and require all provinces to centralize the social pooling at the provincial level, a process that was largely completed in 2021.

In theory, the funding sources for the social pool and individual accounts are completely separate. The social pool is funded on a PAYGO basis, with contribution coming from employers. The individual accounts are funded by workers' own contributions. The contributions are invested and the account balance accumulates over time, and thus, these individual accounts should be fully funded all the time. In reality, these two funding sources have been managed as if they are indistinguishable, due to the problem of legacy pension debt. The legacy pension debt was created because urban enterprise employees who had retired before and those who would retire soon after the establishment of the current system are also covered by each local government's basic pension plan, even though they and their employers had never paid or would pay very little into either the social pool or individual accounts, as discussed in Chapter 1. That puts significant strain on the current funding source, to the point that annual employer contributions could not cover the annual pension payments in many localities. To make up for this deficit, many local governments pulled funds from individual accounts to pay for the benefits. That has resulted in so-called empty individual accounts, a topic that is addressed more fully in Chapter 4. At the time when this new pension plan was established, there was no official valuation of how big this legacy debt would be and how it would be paid off, essentially assuming that it would be paid off by a combination of future contributions and possibly government tax revenue transfers.

To the extent that there is a positive balance in the combined social pool, which is still the case at the provincial level in many provinces, the balance is to be invested to earn interest. It is up to the individual pension plan administrators to decide how to invest the pension plan surplus. Till 2015, most of the surplus funds were invested very conservatively, such as in bank deposits, and thus earned very low returns. The investment returns on these cumulative balances were 2.2%, 2.0%, 2.5%, 2.6%, 2.4%, 2.9%, and 3.1% from 2009 to 2015, respectively, even lower than the inflation rates in these years (MOHRSS, 2016).

Probably as a result of such low investment returns, in 2015, the State Council issued the "Measures for Basic Pension Fund Investment Management" to standardize the investment of pension funds. This rule also applies to the investment management of basic pension funds in the other two plans for public employees and urban and rural residents. Following are some of the main provisions of this measure:

1) The provincial-level government is the trustor of the basic pension fund. All surplus funds within a province should be pooled at the provincial level for investment purposes.
2) The trustor will enter into a trust investment contract with a trustee, an institution established by the government and approved by the State Council. The most important responsibility of the trustee is to design an investment strategy for the pension assets.
3) The trustee will sign a contract with a custody institution (a commercial bank), responsible for the safekeeping of the pension assets.
4) The trustee will also sign a contract with investment companies to manage the investment of pension assets.
5) The measure also sets the following restrictions on the investment:

   A) The assets can only be invested within China. Investable products include bank deposits, fixed-income securities such as central government, local government and corporate debt, equities, and major national construction projects.
   B) Investment in short-term (less than one year) bank deposits and other cash-equivalent products cannot be less than 5% of the portfolio.
   C) Investment in long-term (with maturity over one year) fixed-income securities cannot be more than 135% of the portfolio's net assets.
   D) No more than 30% of the portfolio can be invested in equity and equity-like products.
   E) Investment in major national construction projects cannot be more than 20% of the portfolio.

6) The trustee will keep 1% of the annual return in a reserve fund until the fund balance reaches 5% of the pension fund, as a cushion against future investment loss.

2.3.2 Enterprise annuities for urban enterprise workers

When the central government first officially established enterprise annuities in 2004, it also published the "Trial Measures for the Management of Enterprise Annuity Funds". It was replaced by the "Measures for the Management of Enterprise Annuity Funds" in 2011. To provide enterprise annuities to their employees, enterprises must have participated in the basic pension plan for urban workers and also have the financial capacity to do so. The main provisions of the measures are similar to those that govern the basic pension plan investment, with some minor differences:

1) The company and enterprise annuity participants are the trustors of the enterprise annuity fund.

2) The trustors select a trustee to supervise the fund. However, the trustee can be either an existing government-approved legal trust institution, such as a pension management company, or an enterprise annuity fund council (or governing board) formed by the company itself. The members of the council represent both the company and employees, and they can also be outside professionals. At least one third of the members must be company employees. The most important supervisory responsibility is to design an investment strategy for the enterprise annuity fund.

3) The trustee must also appoint an administrator to perform the routine management duties of the fund, such as collecting contributions into individual accounts and distributing benefit to retirees, appointing a custodian (typically a commercial bank) for safekeeping of pension assets, and appointing an investment company to manage the investment of fund assets.

4) While the measures set the restrictions on investment, they were amended by a notice issued by the MOHRSS in 2013, titled the "Notice on Expanding the Investment Scope of Enterprise Annuity Funds". This notice of 2013 was again replaced by another one issued at the end of 2020 by the MOHRSS, titled the "Notice on Adjusting the Annuity Investment Scope".

A) Assets can only be invested inside China and Hong Kong (only inside China prior to 2020).

B) At least 5% of the assets must be invested in highly liquid assets such as deposits, central bank notes, and short-term bond repos, as well as money market funds. No more than 40% of the fund assets can be invested in bond repurchase agreements.

C) Investment in fixed-income securities, convertible bonds, and bond funds cannot exceed 135% of the fund assets.

D) A maximum of 40% (30% prior to 2020) of assets can be invested in stocks, investment-linked insurance products, and equity funds.

E) Investment in commercial bank wealth management products, trust products, infrastructure debt investment plans, or special asset management plans may not exceed 30% of the net value of the fund assets. In particular, the proportion of investment in trust products must not exceed 10% of the fund assets.

As can be seen, the investment restrictions for enterprise annuity funds are fairly similar to those for basic pension plans. One major difference is that as of 2021, enterprise annuity funds are allowed to invest more in the stock market than the basic pension plans, 40% vs. 30%. The other difference is that no investment in national infrastructure projects is allowed for enterprise annuity funds. Figure 2.1 shows the national average annual investment return on enterprise annuity funds from 2007, the first year such data were available, to 2021 (MOHRSS, 2022). The average annualized rate of return over this period was 7.17%. While there is no benchmark to measure against this average rate of return since no enterprise annuity funds set an expected rate of

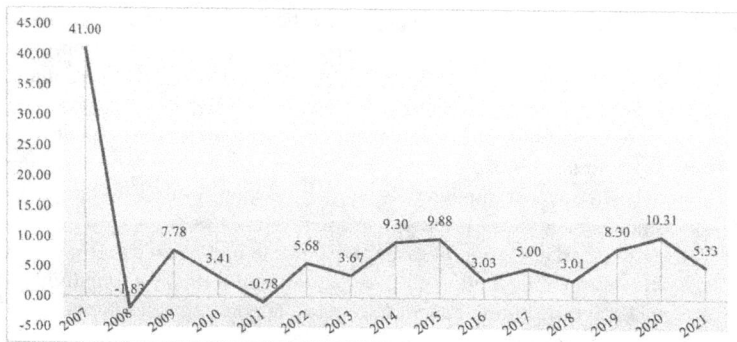

Figure 2.1 Annual Investment Return (%)

Source: MOHRSS. 2021 Enterprise Annuity Funds Statistical Abstract.

return due to the defined contribution nature of this fund, it was higher than the returns achieved by the basic pension plans, at least from 2009 to 2015, when comparable data were available.

2.3.3   *Public employee pension plan occupational annuities*

In 2016, the MOHRSS and the MOF issued the "Interim Measures for the Management of Occupational Annuity Funds". The overall setup of an occupational annuity fund is fairly similar to that of an enterprise annuity fund, such as the requirement of a trustee, administrator, custodian, and investment companies, and the relationships among these parties. There are, however, a few important differences. One difference is that instead of appointing an administrator for an enterprise annuity fund for routine administrator duties, this role is fulfilled by an agent for the occupational annuity fund, defined as a pension management center of the central government and provincial social insurance agencies. The agent also has another important responsibility, which is to form a selection committee to select a trustee, with committee members from the human resources and social security department and the finance department. The role of trustee is fulfilled by a government-approved legal trust institution, but no pension council is formed by the government employers as an alternative, as in the case of enterprise annuity funds. More than one occupational annuity fund can be formed by the central government agent and each of the provincial agents. What this means is that the management of occupational annuity funds is centralized at the provincial level, rather than at the local city or county level. The restrictions on the occupational annuity fund investment are the same as those for the enterprise annuity funds. In 2021, the MOHRSS reported that the investment income on occupational annuity funds amounted to CNY 93 billion.[10] When compared to the fund balance of CNY 1.29 trillion at the end of 2020, that implies an investment return of roughly 7%.

2.3.4 *Urban and rural residents' individual pension plan accounts*

The rule issued by the State Council in 2015, the "Measures for Basic Pension Fund Investment Management" with regard to the management of basic pension funds, also applies to the management of this pension plan's individual accounts. The balance in the individual accounts should be centralized at the provincial level and invested so that the value of the account can appreciate over time. In 2021, the MOHRSS and the MOF issued the "Notice on Standardizing the Book-Keeping Interest Rate for the Individual Accounts of Urban and Rural Residents' Basic Pension Plan". It is up to the provincial government to set the book-keeping interest rate annually, and it needs to be higher than the one-year deposit rate. Since most if not all the provinces now invest the individual account balance, that means the book-keeping rate is loosely tied to the investment return, possibly with the aim of smoothing out the investment return over time. As a result, the book-keeping rate varies from one province to another and from year to year. For example, Qinghai province set this rate at 3.81% in 2022, whereas Guangdong province set it at 2.3% in 2022.[11]

2.4 The National Social Security Fund

The National Social Security Fund (NSSF) was established by the central government in 2000. Despite its title including "social security", which can also include health, unemployment, and disability insurance, the NSSF was founded primarily for the public pension scheme. In anticipation of the population ageing in China in the 21st century and thus the growing pressure for funding pension benefits and the resulting funding gap, primarily in the pension plan for urban enterprise workers, the central government decided to establish this fund as a strategic reserve fund. In other words, it is an alternative source of funding for the basic pension plan for urban enterprise workers and, to a lesser extent, for urban and rural residents. Although the circumstances under which the funds in NSSF can be used to pay for basic pension benefits were never clearly laid out in the regulation establishing the NSSF, it is assumed that in the future when the basic pension plans nationwide can no longer pay the current year basic pension benefits promised with current year revenue and all the accumulated surpluses have been exhausted to cover the annual funding gap, the NSSF then can be tapped to pay for the funding deficit. In its first 20 years of existence, this fund was called upon just once to help out with a funding shortage in the basic pension plan. In 2020, in the aftermath of the COVID outbreak and its effect on the economy, the central government withdrew CNY 50 billion from the NSSF to cover part of the funding deficit in the basic pension plan.[12] Given the long-term importance of this fund to the financing of basic pension plans in China, there is a need to know how the NSSF has been funded and managed since its inception.

When the NSSF was first created, the central government also created the National Council for the Social Security Fund (NCSSF) to manage this fund. The fund was seeded with CNY 20 billion of revenue transfer from the central government's budget in 2000. For the first few years of its existence, its primary source of revenue was central government revenue transfers, although the amount was somewhat volatile. Because the sole purpose of NSSF is to serve as a strategic reserve fund, the goal from the very beginning was to grow the fund by investing the funds transferred in from the central government. Therefore, investment management has been one of the most, if not the most important, responsibilities, of the NCSSF. Because of the importance of investment, the MOF issued a document in 2001 regulating the NCSSF's investment management, titled the "Interim Measures on the National Social Security Fund's Investment Management". It was later supplemented by the "Interim Provisions on the National Social Security Fund's Overseas Investment Management" in 2006, and the "Interim Measures for the Administration of Loans and Investments in Trusts by the National Social Security Fund" in 2014, followed by a revised version in 2016. Between these documents, the following are some of the main provisions with regard to NSSF's investment management:

1) The principles of investment are safety, liquidity, and return, in that order, with an emphasis on safety.
2) NCSSF forms an expert selection committee, including independent professionals, to select investment managers and custodians.
3) The restrictions on investment are as follows:

   A) Bank deposits and government bonds combined should be no less than 50% of assets. At least 10% must be invested in bank deposits.
   B) The limit for corporate bond investment is 10%.
   C) The limit on equity investment is 40%.
   D) The limit on overseas investment is 20%, as of 2006.
   E) NSSF can also make loans directly to major infrastructure projects. The debtors should have good credit quality and be state-run enterprises.

Compared to the investment restrictions for basic pension plans, there are two major differences. First, the limit on equity investment is higher for the NSSF, and second, the NSSF is allowed to invest overseas. One important reason for the first difference is that the investment horizon is much longer for the NSSF than for basic pension plan funds. As it serves as a strategic reserve, no funds are expected to be spent for many years to come, and thus, it can afford to take on more investment risk to grow the fund's value. The basic pension plans, however, have to make annual payments, some of the cumulative balances will be called upon to cover some annual deficits in the near future, and thus, the investment horizon is shorter, leading to lower investment risk. Overseas investment entails foreign exchange, a prerogative enjoyed at this point only by a fund established by the central government.

As of the end of 2021, about 91% assets were invested inside China and 9% were invested overseas; about 34% of assets were invested directly by the NCSSF and 66% of assets were entrusted to outside investment managers for investment (NCSSF, 2022). Figure 2.2 shows the annual investment return on the fund from 2001 through 2021.

The annualized rate of return over this 20-year period was 8.3%. This average return was higher than that for the enterprise annuity funds, although over different time frames. Part of the reason could be the greater investment risks taken on by the NSSF. It could also be due to the fact that the NSSF is bigger than all the separate enterprise annuity funds. It could benefit from economy of scale, in terms of potentially more efficient asset allocation, overseas investment, and lower management cost, as in the case of in-house investment management. This is probably part of the reason behind the notice issued by the MOHRSS in 2020 to allow enterprise annuity funds to increase the allocation to equity from 30% to 40% of assets.

After 15 years of operation, the State Council finally issued a formal decree in 2016 called the "Regulations on the National Social Security Fund" on how to regulate all aspects of the operation of the NSSF. While the regulations did

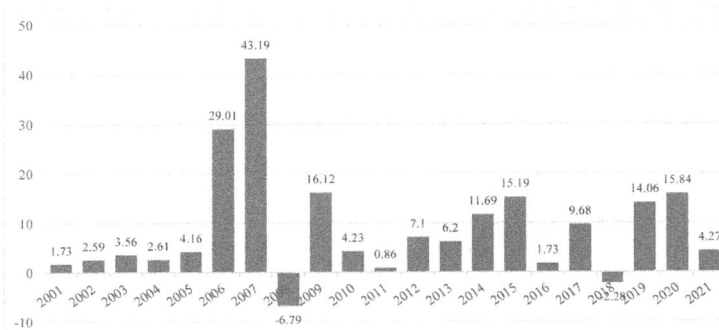

Figure 2.2 NSSF's Annual Investment Return (%)

Source: NCSSF's Report on the NSSF's Annual Investment Return, available at www.ssf.gov.cn/portal/xxgk/fdzdgknr/cwbg/czbr/webinfo/2022/08/1662443045389432.htm.

not break any new ground, with one exception, their purpose was to formalize, at a higher government level, the role of the NSSF, its financing sources, and how it should be regulated. It confirmed the role of the NSSF as a strategic reserve for the country's basic pension plans. It also officially designated the four revenue sources the NSSF will receive: (a) central government revenue transfer, (b) investment income, (c) transfer of equity shares of state-owned public companies, and (d) any other revenue source designated by the State Council. In recent years, the only other major revenue source has been a portion of public lottery proceeds designated for the NSSF.

While state-owned enterprise equity transfers have been going on for some time, in 2017, the State Council issued the "Implementation Plan for Transferring Part of State-Owned Capital to Fortify Social Security Funds". The plan calls for transferring 10% of the equities of state-owned public companies. The purpose is to provide another source of long-term funding for the NSSF. The plan makes it clear that the major source of income from this transfer of equities is not the resale of equities but rather the dividends earned on the equities.

With the annual infusion of revenue transfer from various sources and the positive investment return earned in most years, the size of the NSSF has been growing steadily since its establishment in 2000. Table 2.9 presents the annual revenue transfer and growth of NSSF since 2000.

Of the total fund balance of CNY 2.598 trillion at the end of 2021, CNY 1.571 trillion was earned through investment, and CNY 1.027 trillion was revenue transfer from the central government. Of the revenue transfer, CNY 355 billion came from the general budget, CNY 390 billion were lottery proceeds, and CNY 284 billion were from the transfer of equity shares of state-owned enterprises.

Table 2.9 Revenue Transfer and Fund Balance of the NSSF (in billions)

Year	Fund Balance	Revenue Transfer	Year	Fund Balance	Revenue Transfer
2000		20.0	2011	772.8	48.3
2001		59.5	2012	893.3	52.6
2002	124.2	41.6	2013	991.1	55.4
2003	132.5	4.9	2014	1,240.8	55.2
2004	171.1	27.9	2015	1,508.3	70.6
2005	195.4	22.9	2016	1,604.3	70.1
2006	272.4	57.4	2017	1,830.2	59.8
2007	414.0	30.8	2018	1,810.5	57.4
2008	480.4	32.7	2019	2,137.7	46.5
2009	692.8	82.6	2020	2,459.1	31.4
2010	780.9	63.4	2021	2,598.1	36.1

Source: Annual financial reports on the NSSF issued by the NCSSF, www.ssf.gov.cn/portal/xxgk/fdzdgknr/cwbg/A00100308index_1.htm.

As mentioned earlier, the regulation issued in 2016 did break new ground in one way. For the first time, the NCSSF was officially allowed to accept provincial governments' requests to invest on their behalf the surplus funds in their provinces' basic pension plans. While the NCSSF had invested for Guangdong and Shandong provinces in the past as a pilot program, this was the first time all provinces could ask the NCSSF to invest for them. This was primarily for two reasons: (1) to benefit from the economy of scale of the NSSF and (2) to benefit from the relatively high and steady return achieved by the NCSSF so far. At the end of 2021, assets under the management of NCSSF on behalf of basic pension plans amounted to CNY 1.46 trillion.[13] As the total balance of all 31 mainland provinces' basic pension plan was CNY 5.26 trillion at the end of 2021, this means that about 28% of that total balance was contracted out to the NCSSF for investment management.

It should be noted that since the rules on investment restrictions on the NSSF and basic pension plan funds are different, as can be seen from the discussion earlier, the NCSSF has to invest the funds entrusted to it separately from its own funds and use different asset allocation strategy that meets the restrictions on basic pension plan funds. It is thus not a surprise that the annual rate of return should also be different. For the five years between 2017 and 2021 when such comparable data were available, the returns on NSSF funds were 9.68%, -2.28%, 14.06%, 15.84%, and 4.27%, as Figure 2.2 shows. For these same five years, the returns on basic pension plan funds were 5.23%, 2.56%, 9.03%, 10.95%, and 4.88%.[14] It is noteworthy that the safer investment strategy led to less volatility in return for basic pension plans but also a lower average return over a multiyear period.

2.5 Central Government's adjustment mechanism

Another major governance issue in recent years has been the central government's pension fund adjustment mechanism. In 2018, the State Council issued the "Notice on Establishing the Central Government Adjustment System for Enterprise Workers Old-Age Insurance Fund". It went into effect on July 1, 2018. This was a major step towards establishing a nationwide pension fund for enterprise workers. The purpose of this adjustment mechanism was to transfer funds from provinces with annual surplus funds to provinces with major deficits. Due to the fragmentation of basic pension plans for urban workers, as discussed earlier, and due to differences in the demographics of participants in different provinces, some provinces have had large annual surpluses and positive fund balances in their pension plans, whereas other provinces have had just the opposite. The adjustment mechanism is to correct this imbalance. It involves two steps: first, how much funds the central government should collect from each province and second, how much the central government should distribute back to each province, all based on a formula.[15]

The formula for submission of funds from each province is as follows: the amount to be submitted to the central government is equal to the following:

(The average salary of employee in a province * 90%) * the number of employees that should be covered by the basic pension system in the province * a submission ratio.

The submission ratio was first set at 3% in 2018. It was raised to 3.5% in 2019 and further to 4% in 2020. The higher the submission ratio, the more a province will have to submit, and thus, the central government will have more funds to redistribute nationwide. Theoretically speaking, when the submission ratio reaches 100%, there will be a unified nationwide pension plan for all enterprise workers.

After the central government collects all the funds submitted from the province, it disburses the total collected funds to each province based on a formula. The amount to be disbursed to each province is equal to the following:

The number of retirees in a province * national average amount to be allocated to a retiree.

The national average amount to be allocated to a retiree is equal to the following:

The total amount collected from all provinces/the number of retirees nationwide.

Table 2.10 shows the funds submitted from and disbursed to each province in 2019.

In total, close to CNY 630 billion was collected in 2019 by the central government and distributed back to the provinces. However, about CNY 367 billion, or 58% of the total amount collected, came from just seven provinces (Beijing, Fujian, Guangdong, Jiangsu, Shandong, Shanghai, and Zhejiang). These seven provinces received back from the central government about CNY 151 billion. These seven provinces were the only net contributors to the system, to the tune of CNY 216 billion, and all other provinces were net receivers of these funds, with Liaoning province being the biggest beneficiary of this adjustment mechanism. As a matter of fact, three of the top four recipients of funds were the three northeastern provinces. On the other hand, all the net contributors, with the exception of the capital city of Beijing, are prosperous provinces along the coast, with Guangdong province being the biggest contributor, accounting for a third of the net contribution.

This is not a coincidence. As a matter of fact, this geographical distribution of net contributors and biggest net recipients is the reason behind this

Table 2.10 Central Government Adjustment System in 2019 (in billions)

Province	Total Revenue	Submission	Disbursement	Difference
Beijing	243.2	51.3	17.1	34.2
Tianjin	75.4	11.0	11.6	(0.6)
Heibei	118.9	15.1	17.9	(2.8)
Shanxi	76.9	8.5	10.6	(2.1)
Inner Mongolia	62.0	7.1	15.1	(8.0)
Liaoning	191.6	17.0	62.7	(45.7)
Jilin	74.5	7.7	19.6	(11.9)
Heilongjiang	123.3	8.9	52.2	(43.3)
Shanghai	246.6	43.0	32.4	10.6
Jiangsu	275.3	62.3	48.3	14.0
Zhijiang	237.2	49.7	38.4	11.3
Anhui	106.1	14.2	15.5	(1.3)
Fujian	63.0	20.5	9.3	11.2
Jiangxi	72.7	13.2	17.4	(4.2)
Shandong	191.2	44.1	35.9	8.2
Henan	126.3	21.9	22.6	(0.7)
Hubei	148.6	19.9	31.9	(12.0)
Hunan	119.2	13.8	17.0	(3.2)
Guangdong	401.1	96.5	34.8	61.7
Guangxi	66.8	9.5	10.8	(1.3)
Hainan	23.4	3.2	3.4	(0.2)
Chongqing	99.8	17.0	18.8	(1.8)
Sichuan	206.1	25.7	33.9	(8.2)
Guizhou	46.2	9.4	9.4	0.0
Yunnan	56.4	9.7	9.7	0.0
Tibet	4.5	0.8	0.8	0.0
Shaanxi	88.9	11.1	11.9	(0.8)
Gansu	38.4	5.4	6.4	(1.0)
Qinghai	13.2	1.6	2.2	(0.6)
Ningxia	18.9	2.5	3.4	(0.9)
Xinjiang	52.6	6.4	6.5	(0.1)
Xinjiang Construction Corp	24.9	2.3	2.9	(0.6)
Total		630.3	630.3	

Source: MOF, Central Government Budget, http://yss.mof.gov.cn/2020zyys/.

whole adjustment mechanism. The provinces along the coast are the most prosperous in China for many reasons, especially due to their export-oriented economies and new industry such as high tech. Therefore, these provinces attract a lot of young working people coming from other parts of the country to work in these provinces, thus increasing the number of people contributing to the pension system. At the same time, the three northeastern provinces, Liaoning, Jilin, and Heilongjiang, are a bastion of heavy industries that laid the foundation for China's industrialization in the past. However, they have not benefited as much from the modern economy and have experienced much slower economic growth than the coastal region. They have a lot of retirees from these heavy industries, they have not attracted young people, and some of the young people in these provinces have left for the booming coastal provinces. This creates a significant variation in the dependency ratio across these provinces, but a high dependency ratio is essential to the fiscal health of a pension plan funded on a PAYGO basis. In Guangdong province, there were eight workers to each retiree, whereas in Heilongjiang, only 1.3 workers supported one retiree in 2017, according to the MOHRSS, when the national average was 2.73 in that year.[16]

This pattern of fund collection and disbursement was the same in 2020 and 2021, except that the total amount collected and disbursed was larger, reaching CNY 832 billion in 2021. The seven provinces were still the only net contributors to the system in 2021.

2.6 Nationally coordinated basic pension plan for urban enterprise workers

The central government's pension adjustment mechanism was meant to be a temporary step on China's march to a nationally unified pension plan. Thus, after only three years in practice, it was discontinued in 2022. On February 22, 2022, the MOHRSS announced that the national coordination of basic pension plans was finally initiated in January of 2022,[17] based on the fact that all provinces had centralized the coordination of basic pension plans at the provincial level. The new system is based on five standardizations:

- Standardization of pension benefit policy, including contribution rate, base, pension benefit items, and adjustment.
- Standardization of the management system for collecting and disbursing pension funds.
- Standardization of a mechanism for the central and local governments to be separately responsible for pension benefit cost.
- Standardization of service management information system and promotion of a nationally coordinated information system.
- Standardization of the mechanism for assessing the performance of provincial governments.

However, such national coordination does not mean the central government collects all pension contributions nationwide and then disburses benefits nationally based on a unified pension benefit formula, which are the hallmarks of a national pension plan like the Social Security system in the United States. It turns out this is still an intermediate step towards that ultimate goal. It was more like a stepped-up central government pension fund adjustment mechanism in practice between 2019 and 2021. Instead of collecting funds, net of distribution, and only from provinces with annual surpluses, the new system works as follows:

- Funds will be collected from provinces with a cumulative pension surplus, even if they may already have an annual deficit in their pension financing.
- The funds to be collected by the central government are based on a percentage: total national annual pension deficit/total national cumulative pension surpluses. This percentage is then applied to the cumulative pension surplus of each province.
- The funds thus collected are then distributed to provinces with an annual deficit in pension financing based on another percentage. This percentage varies between two types of provinces based on whether they have a cumulative pension surplus or not, with the percentage being higher for those with no cumulative pension surplus.
- However, the funds distributed this way will not cover the entire annual pension deficit of each province. The local government is supposed to budget with its own funds to cover the remaining pension deficit.

Table 2.11 shows the results of this new system.

Comparing Table 2.11 with Table 2.10, it is obvious that under the new system, more provinces contributed into the national pool and fewer provinces

Table 2.11 2022 National Reallocation of Basic Pension Plan Revenues (in billions)

Province	Basic Plan Total Revenue	Collected	Disbursed
Beijing	329.4	32.3	
Tianjin	92.7		5.4
Heibei	137.3		0.4
Shanxi	94.2	0.3	
Inner Mongolia	76.1		16.6
Liaoning	234.3		82.0
Jilin	83.3		23.8
Heilongjiang	142.7		82.2
Shanghai	315.5	6.8	
Jiangsu	351.4	17.9	
Zhijiang	312.9	9.5	
Anhui	127.9	8.4	
Fujian	76.8	6.7	
Jiangxi	90.8	3.7	
Shandong	244.7		1.5
Henan	152.9	2.4	
Hubei	179.0		3.2
Hunan	130.2	2.3	
Guangdong	578.8	88.5	
Guangxi	90.4	3.1	

(*Continued*)

Table 2.11 (Continued)

Province	Basic Plan Total Revenue	Collected	Disbursed
Hainan	29.3	2.2	
Chongqing	126.7	5.0	
Sichuan	269.6	8.7	
Guizhou	57.4	4.7	
Yunnan	70.9	6.2	
Tibet	6.3	1.1	
Shaanxi	107.7	3.8	
Gansu	45.7		1.2
Qinghai	18.2		1.3
Ningxia	21.6	0.3	
Xinjiang	64.7	3.8	
Xinjiang Construction Corp	29.8		0.1
Total	4,689.2	217.5	217.6

Source: MOF, available at http://yss.mof.gov.cn/2022zyczys/202203/t20220324_3797594.htm.

received funds from this pool. This means that some provinces with annual funding deficits still have cumulative positive balances in their pension plans that they can draw on to offset some of the annual funding deficit.

It is also obvious from Tables 2.10 and 2.11 that despite major reform efforts since 2018, China is still at a stage of reallocating funds among provinces, and thus, Chinese public pension plans still remain fragmented and will require more fundamental reforms from the central government to make them into a unified nationwide public pension plan.

Notes

1 The data are collected from the notices issued MOHRSS and MOF in various years. For example, the notice issued in 2020 for the pension benefit increase can be found at www.gov.cn/zhengce/zhengceku/202004/19/content_5504190.htm.
2 MOHRSS. 2005. Notice of Promotion Guideline on the Decision on Improving Enterprise Employees' Basic Pension System. Issued by the State Council. Available at www.elinklaw.com/zsglmobile/lawView.aspx?id=73131.
3 Chinese Central Government. 2018. Urban and Rural Residents' Minimum Base Pension Increases to CNY 88 Per Month. Available at www.gov.cn/xinwen/2018-05/13/content_5290643.htm.
4 Chinese Central Government. 2021. Will Urban and Rural Residents' Pension Increase Again Over the Next Five Years? Available at www.gov.cn/fuwu/2021-03/16/content_5593351.htm.
5 For Shanghai, see the directive issued by the Shanghai Municipal government, titled Shanghai Municipal Urban and Rural Residents Basic Pension Insurance Methods, effective May 1, 2019. Available at http://sh.sina.com.cn/news/m/2019-04-25/detail-ihvhiewr8223961.shtml; for Henan, see the news release by the central government. Available at www.gov.cn/xinwen/2019-01/31/content_5362801.htm.

6 The annual bulletins of MOHRSS are available at www.mohrss.gov.cn/SYrlzyhs hbzb/zwgk/szrs/tjgb/.

7 However, the MOHRSS does not officially break down the numbers (including financial data) between urban enterprise workers and public-sector employees.

8 Information on government subsidies was discontinued after 2017.

9 This ratio of 20:1, derived from this calculation at an aggregate level, turns out to be very similar to official data in the "Chinese Social Insurance Development Annual Report" published in 2016 by the MOHRSS. In 2015, the average monthly pension for retired urban enterprise workers was CNY 2,251, or 19.3 times the average monthly pension of CNY 116.7 for retired urban and rural residents.

10 MOHRSS. Annual Bulletin for 2021.

11 For Qinhai, see https://m12333.cn/policy/krsy.html. For Guangdong, see http://hrss.gd.gov.cn/gkmlpt/content/3/3991/post_3991954.html#4034.

12 MOF. 2021. Summary Report on 2020 Central and Local Budget Execution and 2021 Central and Local Budget Proposals (in Chinese). Available at www.mof.gov.cn/zhengwuxinxi/caizhengxinwen/202103/t20210306_3666607.htm.

13 NCSSF. 2022. NCSSF 2021 Annual Report on the Operation of Entrusted Basic Pension Funds. Available at www.ssf.gov.cn/portal/xxgk/fdzdgknr/cwbg/yljjndbg/webinfo/2022/09/1664865877855617.htm.

14 The data are from the NCSSF's annual report on the operation of entrusted basic pension funds. Available at www.ssf.gov.cn/portal/xxgk/fdzdgknr/cwbg/yljjndbg/A0010030802index_1.htm.

15 In practice, the central government may simply calculate a net collection amount based on the formula for each province. If this net amount is positive, the province will submit that amount to the central government. Otherwise, a province will receive a net transfer from the central government.

16 The data came from the MOHRSS in a news release on June 13, 2018, titled "MOHRSS: Gradually Improving the System, and Achieving National Coordination of Pension Plan ASAP". Available at www.chinanews.com.cn/m/cj/2018/06-13/8536942.shtml.

17 See the news release by the Chinese central government on February 25, 2022, titled "National Coordination of Basic Pension Plan for Enterprise Workers Started in January". Available at www.gov.cn/xinwen/202202/25/content_5675550.htm.

References

Fang, Hanming, and Jin Feng. 2018. The Chinese Pension System. NBER Working Paper Series. Available at www.nber. org/papers/e25088.

MOHRSS. 2016. Chinese Social Insurance Development Annual Report 2015. Beijing: China Labor and Social Security Publishing House.

MOHRSS. 2022. 2021 Enterprise Annuity Funds Statistical Abstract. Available at www.mohrss.gov.cn/shbxjjjds/SHBXJDSzhengcewenjian/202203/W02022031169 4382790812.pdf.

NCSSF. 2022. NCSSF Annual Financial Report on NSSF for 2021. Available at www.ssf.gov.cn/portal/xxgk/fdzdgknr/cwbg/sbjjndbg/webinfo/2022/08/166238 1965418407.htm.

3 A case study of three provinces

3.1 Introduction

As a result of the continuous effort of the central government, China's pension system has become increasingly centralized in the last two decades. At present, the "Decision on Improving Enterprise Employees' Basic Pension System" (Document 38, 2005), the "State Council Guidelines on Developing an Urban Residents' Old-Age Social Insurance Pilot Project" (2011), and the "Decision on the Reform of the Pension System for Civil Servants and Employees of Public Institutions" (2015), all issued by the State Council, constitute the authoritative legislative documents for the three national pension plans. These official documents contain detailed guidance and regulations that all subnational governments must follow when designing, implementing, and managing their pension plans. It turns out that many pension policies in China are nationwide and mandatory in nature, leaving the Human Resources and Social Security Departments (HRSS) of subnational governments with little room for policy discretion. For example, Document 38 stipulated the most important aspects of the pension plan for all urban enterprise workers, including the range of coverage, contribution rate, level of social pooling, enterprise annuity, and so forth. In addition, from time to time, the State Council and the MOHRSS of China may issue amendments, measures, decisions, or plans that also have the overarching legislative power in governing the pension plans. For instance, the State Council promulgated the "Comprehensive Plan on Reducing Social Insurance Contribution Rates" in 2019 to lower the mandatory employer contribution from 20% to 16% of the employee's wage without a reduction in pension benefits. For these reasons, it is not surprising that the pension plans in different regions of China bear considerable similarities.

Nevertheless, these similarities should not be exaggerated because there are still noticeable variances in the pension management of each subnational government of China for at least three reasons. First, the pension plans in China were traditionally administered by prefectures or even lower levels of governments, so the design and governance of local pension plans were highly

DOI: 10.4324/9781003091974-3

fragmented in the past. Although the central government has taken effective measures to build a unified national system by combining local plans, it may take a long time to achieve that goal, and hence, the many different pension features inherited from the previous plans are likely to persist for some time. Second, in certain policy areas, the official legislative documents of the central government have explicitly left some room for provincial governments' discretion. For instance, Document 38 specifically allows "each region to put forward a specific benefit adjustment plan in accordance with the local actual situation". Regarding the base pension benefit for urban and rural residents, the current national policy clearly states that while "The central government determines the minimum standard for basic pensions . . . local governments may appropriately raise the basic pension standard in accordance with the actual situation".[1] Such flexibility is necessary for subnational governments to implement their pension policies smoothly during China's period of transition towards a unified national system. Last, the current national documents do not cover every aspect of pension administration. For example, the current national pension policies provide little guidance for provincial and local governments on how to deal with legacy debts and how to divide the financial burden of funding the social pool or covering pension deficits between provincial and prefecture-level governments. Therefore, each subnational government may need to come up with its own plan to fill in such policy blanks.

To explore the variances in pension administration among different regions of China, we selected three representative provinces in China and conducted a case study to compare how the three provincial-level governments design and administer their pension plans. The three selected provinces are Guangdong, Heilongjiang, and Sichuan in Southern, Northeastern, and Western China, respectively. Besides the geographical location, other criteria for the case selection include average wage, economic structure, labor force characteristics, and current pension situation. As Figure 3.1 shows, Guangdong is one of the richest provinces in China, whereas Heilongjiang is one of the poorest, and Sichuan lies somewhere in between. In addition, there are sharp differences in the economic structure and demographic characteristics among the three provinces: Guangdong is a typical coastal and economically prosperous province that attracts a large number of migrant workers from other parts of the country, Heilongjiang is an economically stagnant province that loses many workers to other provinces, and Sichuan is an inland province with a relatively stable economic structure and a balanced flow of labor. There is no doubt that these sharp differences have influential impacts on the management and health of the respective pension plans. While the three provinces may not be sufficient to cover the diverse reality of the entire pension system in China, it is our hope that this case study will provide a fuller picture of the unique challenges facing each subnational government and also help to probe into the reasons why different governments have adopted different pension strategies.

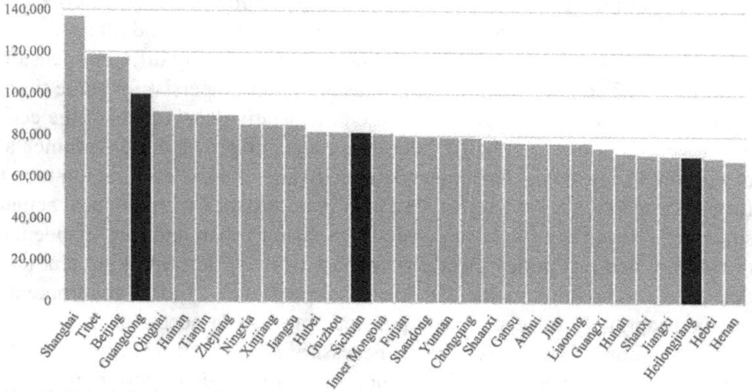

Figure 3.1 Provincial-Level Weighted Average Annual Wage for Urban Workers in 2022

3.2 Guangdong: An economically prosperous province with a net inflow of labor

Located on the southern coast and next to Hong Kong and Macao, Guangdong is one of the most populous and prosperous provinces in China. For more than two thousand years, Guangdong has been the most important foreign trade center, and its capital city, Guangzhou, is the only seaport that has remained open to the outside world throughout the history of the country. Since the "reform and opening" policy implemented in the early 1980s, Guangdong has been one of the provinces with the largest economies as measured by regional GDP. According to the National Bureau of Statistics, Guangdong has consistently ranked in 1st place in terms of total GDP among Chinese provincial-level administrative divisions for the past 30 years. In 2021, the total GDP of Guangdong reached CNY 12.44 trillion, or USD 1.92 trillion, surpassing the national GDP of Korea or Russia.

However, the rapid economic growth and the large GDP are not the whole story. One distinctive feature of the economic development of the province is the remarkable economic disparity among different regions of the province. Traditionally, the 21 prefecture-level cities of Guangdong can be divided into four major economic areas (see Figure 3.2): Eastern (Chaozhou, Shantou, Jieyang, and Shanwei), Northern (Meizhou, Heyuan, Shaoguan, Qingyuan, and Yunfu), Western (Zhanjiang, Maoming, and Yangjiang), and Pearl River Delta (Zhaoqing, Foshan, Jiangmen, Guangzhou, Zhuhai, Zhongshan, Dongguan, Shenzhen, and Huizhou). While the Pearl River Delta region (especially Guangzhou and Shenzhen) is one of the most developed metropolitan areas in the world with a per-capita GDP of more than USD 20,000, the other three

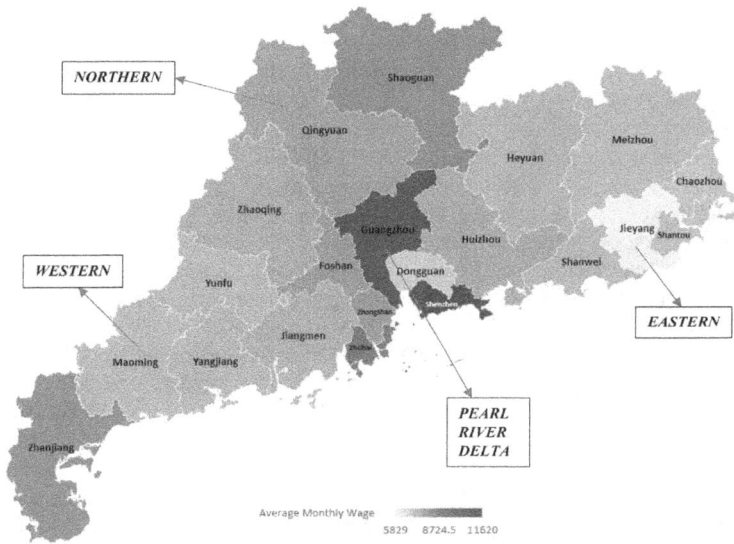

Figure 3.2 Average Monthly Wage for the 21 Prefecture-Level Cities of Guangdong in 2020

regions of the province are much less prosperous with per-capita GDPs similar to those of many inland provinces. In fact, the Pearl River Delta region accounted for more than 80% of the total GDP of Guangdong in 2021. As a direct consequence of this dramatic economic disparity, the average wage and the associated living standard also vary dramatically from one region to another within the province: in 2020, the highest average monthly wage for prefecture-level cities was CNY 11,620 (Shenzhen), whereas the lowest was only CNY 5,829 (Jieyang).

Another important feature of Guangdong is its unique demographic structure. As of November 1, 2020, the resident population (defined as the population actually living in the jurisdiction for more than six months, with or without Hukous) of Guangdong province was 126 million, increasing from 104 million in 2010.[2] However, a closer look at the most recent demographic figures for the province reveals at least three salient issues that are important for its pension management. First, the vast majority of residents are concentrated in the Pearl River Delta region, accounting for about 61.9% of the total population in 2020. This has been a continuing upward trend, increasing from 53.9% in 2010. By contrast, the resident population of the Eastern, Northern, and Western regions only accounted for 13.0%, 12.5%, and 12.6%, respectively. Second, both the size and the proportion of the mobile population from other provinces (defined as the population with Hukous in other provinces who are living in Guangdong for more than six months) continue to grow fast. Since the inception of the economic reforms in the 1980s, a large labor force from other parts of the country has flowed into Guangdong, but the majority of them were temporary workers due to the strict Hukou system in China. As many municipalities have made their Hukous more accessible to these people in recent years, Guangdong has been absorbing more interprovincial mobile workers. Between 2010 and 2020, the total mobile population from other provinces increased from 21.5 million to 29.6 million, accounting for 23.5% of the total resident population. People of working age account for more than 90% of the mobile population, with a dramatically higher male-to-female ratio (145:100) than the national average (105:100). Last and more important, the ageing process of the population of Guangdong has begun to accelerate. From 2010 to 2020, the proportion of the population aged over 60 increased from 9.7% to 12.4%, while the proportion of the workforce aged between 19 and 59 declined from 73.4% to 68.8%. Owing to the large inflow of workers from other provinces, Guangdong has one of largest workforces between 19 and 59 in absolute terms (86.7 million) and the highest percentage of working people, but the ageing population over 60 has also reached 15.6 million and begun to increase faster. As a result, the overall dependency ratio in the province has dropped from 11.2 in 2010 to 8.5 in 2020.

Although other economic, social, and cultural factors may also be relevant, the great economic disparity among different regions and the unique demographic structure constitute the two most important challenges for pension design and management. For example, due to the dramatic differences in average wage and living standards in different regions within the province, the economic disparity in Guangdong constitutes a huge obstacle to establishing a unified base for pension contributions and benefits. As another example, the basic pension plans funded on a PAYGO basis are under strain as the ageing problem looms large and the dependency ratio begins to decline. Moreover, as a significant portion of the mobile population is young workers from other provinces, Guangdong is facing the challenges of how to transition these people from their old pension plans to current plans and how to compensate the losses of the provinces supplying the workforce.

3.2.1   Basic pension plans for urban enterprise workers and public-sector employees

Guangdong's basic pension plans for urban enterprise workers and public-sector employees have been growing steadily in recent years. From 2016 to 2019, the total number of participants of the two plans declined from 53.92 million to 46.33 million. This was largely because of the government's effort to remove duplicate pension accounts of enterprise workers from 2017 to 2019.[3] From 2019 to 2021, the total enrollment quickly recovered and climbed to 50.79 million as a result of a continuous inflow of labor force from both the rural areas of Guangdong and other provinces. If we include the enrollment in the urban and rural residents' plan, the total number of pension plan participants in Guangdong was 75.3 million in 2020, accounting for 59.8% of the resident population or 76.8% of the population with Hukous. Considering that 18.85% of the resident population in 2020 was children under 15 years and a small proportion of the population between 15 and 59 (68.8%) were also school students, the three pension plans had already covered the majority of people with Hukous by 2020. However, it is possible that up to 21% of the total residents of Guangdong (with and without Hukous) did not participate in any of the three pension plans, either because they participated in pension plans of other provinces or they deliberately chose not to enroll in any pension plan.

Unlike the variations in the total enrollment, the number of both contributing workers and retirees for the two pension plans grew steadily from 2016 to 2021. As Table 3.1 shows, the number of pension contributors increased by more than 40% from 2016 to 2021, largely because of the rapid growth in resident population (2.2 million per year on average) during this period. At the same time, the number of retirees remained relatively small when compared to that of many other provinces, leading to a much higher dependency ratio than the national average (see Table 2.5). However, as the population of Guangdong started to age, the dependency ratio for the basic pension plan gradually declined from about 5.88 to 5.75 during this period. This downward trend is likely to continue into the future as the whole nation becomes an ageing society with a low fertility rate.[4]

As a result of the increasing average wage and number of contributing workers, the total revenue of the basic pension plans for urban enterprise workers and public-sector employees grew fast from 2016 to 2018. Typically, most pension revenue in Guangdong comes from employers' contributions, whereas only a small portion comes from government subsidy, intergovernmental transfer, interest, etc. For instance, out of the total pension revenue of CNY 308 billion in 2016, 262 billion was collected from contributions, 30.7 billion was from intergovernmental transfers, 13.4 billion was from interest income, 1.76 billion was from government financial subsidies, and 0.48 billion was from other sources. In 2019, two important events occurred that could affect the pension revenue over the long run. One was the transition of pension contribution collecting authority from local HRSSes to tax bureaus, which took effect on January 1. The other was the reduction in the employer's contribution rate from 20% to 16%, which took effect on May 1, 2019. Prior to that year, a large portion of China's private enterprises engaged in a tax-evasion strategy to save on pension contributions by underreporting the actual wages of their employees. According to the China Enterprise Social

Table 3.1 Enrollment and Finance of Basic Pension Plan for Urban Enterprise Workers and Public-Sector Employees in Guangdong

Year	Total Participants (Million)	Contributing Workers (Million)	Retirees (Million)	Dependency Ratio	Total Revenue (Billion)	Total Expenditure (Billion)	Accumulated Balance (Billion)	Net Submission (Billion)
2016	53.92	30.83	5.25	5.88	308.00	194.01	765.26	
2017	52.87	32.53	5.37	5.80	378.80	222.90	924.50	
2018	49.20	33.54	5.59	6.00	449.47	279.14	1,035.32	
2019	46.33				481.09			61.70
2020	48.73	41.62	7.11	5.85	385.81	331.36	1,233.83	64.57
2021	50.79	43.27	7.52	5.75	611.30	348.40	1,411.00	83.04

Source: HRSS of Guangdong Annual Bulletin, various years. Available at http://hrss.gd.gov.cn/zwgk/sjfb/index.html.

Security White Paper (2017),[5] more than 70% of Chinese private enterprises underreported their employees' wages for pension contribution purposes, and about 22.9% of the enterprises always paid their pension contributions at the minimum level (60% of the local average wage) required by the MOHRSS. However, once the pension contributions were collected by the tax agency, the private enterprises could no longer hide the true information on their employees' wages. This implies a much stricter pension collection enforcement, leading to higher pension revenues for both the social pool and individual accounts.[6] As such, despite a 4 percentage point reduction in the employers' contribution rate since 2019, the total revenue continued to grow in 2019. When COVID-19 struck the economy in 2020, Guangdong's pension revenue experienced a large drop by almost CNY 100 billion, but it quickly bounced back in 2021, probably because of the economic recovery and a boom in the labor market of the province.

On the expenditure side, the growing number of retirees and the increase in benefit levels drove the total pension expenditure in Guangdong up from 194 billion in 2016 to 348.4 billion in 2020. As is the case with most other pension funds, the majority of pension expenditure is used to pay pension benefits. For instance, CNY 160.6 billion out of the total expenditure (194 billion) was spent on pension benefits in 2016, while a small portion was transferred to other governments. In recent years, the growth rate in expenditure has seemed to slow down as a consequence of the declining annual pension benefit growth rate as mandated by the MOHRSS and the MOF. Since the second half of 2018, the central government had begun to implement a national adjustment mechanism, resulting in net submissions of CNY 61.7, 65.6, and 83.0 billion for three consecutive years for the province. These huge losses of funds notwithstanding, the total accumulated balance for the two plans almost doubled from 2016 to 2020, ranking 1st in the nation and indicating a very strong and healthy cash flow pattern for the plan.

As mentioned in the previous section, the biggest challenge for Guangdong's public pension management is the enormous disparity in the average wage among the four economic areas of the province. If the province is to set a uniform average wage level for the purpose of social pooling, the higher-income areas will have to subsidize a significant part of the lower-income areas, as a result of the large difference in local wages to which both pension contribution and benefits are tied. To deal with this problem, the government of Guangdong created a transition plan in 2017 to achieve the goal of establishing a provincially unified pension plan by 2025, four years later than 2021 as required by the MOHRSS.[7] According to this plan, the 21 prefecture-level cities are divided into four tiers of cities, roughly reflecting the average income level of each economic region. As Table 3.2 shows, the first tier, consisting of Guangzhou and Shenzhen, typically has an average wage higher than the provincial average, whereas the other three tiers have an average wage lower than the provincial level. During the transition period,

Table 3.2 Average Monthly Wage of the Four City Groups for Social Pooling

	Group/Year	2017–2018	2019–2020	2020–2021	2021–2022	2022–2023
	Weighted average wage for the province	6,071	6,338	6,756	7,647	8,310
1st	Guangzhou, Shenzhen	5,283[9]	7,450	7,880	8,919	No change
2nd	Zhuhai, Foshan, Dongguan, Zhongshan	4,843	5,626	5,855	6,597	No change
3rd	Shantou, Huizhou, Jiangmen, Zhaoqing	4,470	5,210	5,400	6,122	No change
4th	Shaoguan, Heyuan, Meizhou, Shanwei, Yangjiang, Zhanjiang, Maoming, Qingyuan, Chaozhou, Jieyang, Yunfu	4,148	4,874	5,325	6,334	No change

the upper limit of contributions is the same for the whole province, but the lower limit should be calculated based on the average wage of the tier of cities if that average is lower than the provincial average. For example, for the fiscal year for social security purposes from July 1, 2019, to June 30, 2020, the upper limit of contributions was three times the weighted average wage of the province, CNY 19,014 (6,338 × 300%), and the lower limit was 60% of the provincial-level average wage (CNY 6,338 × 60% = 3,803) for the top tier of cities. However, for the 2nd, 3rd, and 4th tiers, the lower bounds were 60% of their own average wages, or CNY 3,376, 3,126, and 2,924, respectively.[8] It is evident that this arrangement allows the employers and employees of lower-income regions to contribute less to the social pool during the transition period. According to this plan, however, the province will gradually merge the four tiers of cities and set a unified lower bound, which is 60% of the provincial average wage, for all regions by 2025.

Consistent with the movement towards a unified provincial-level pension system, Guangdong also took a few other important measures to centralize the administration of previously locally administered pension funds. As stipulated in the "Opinions about Standardizing the Implementation of the Provincial Coordination of the Guangdong's Enterprise Workers' Basic Pension Plan" (2020),[10] Guangdong has begun to standardize both the collection of pension contributions and the expenditure on pension benefits at the provincial level since January 1, 2021. To standardize the collection, the provincial government has set up a special social security account to receive all funds submitted from municipal and county governments, including pension contributions, government subsidies, intergovernmental transfers, interest and investment income, and so forth. Moreover, the municipal and county governments must turn over their account balances accumulated prior to January 1, 2021, in several batches to the provincial special account by December 31, 2030. To standardize the expenditure, the province has required all social security agencies at the municipal or county level to make monthly requests to the HRSS of Guangdong. Upon the approval of the Department of Finance of Guangdong Province, the HRSS will then appropriate necessary funds to local social security agencies for pension payments. With these "Opinions" in place, the local social security agencies in the province no longer have the fiscal authority for pension-related issues, except that they are allowed to retain enough reserves for two months of pension payments. Besides the collection and expenditure, the "Opinions" also laid out detailed measures for standardizing the pension contribution rates, benefit levels, budget-making methods, responsibility sharing mechanisms, and information systems for all municipal and county governments. Overall, as mandated by the central government, Guangdong is quickly moving towards a provincial-level unified pension system. The only two exceptions are the setting of the lower limit of contribution in four tiers of prefecture-level cities, which is scheduled to be phased out in 2025, and the turnover of the accumulated balance from local social security agencies to the provincial special account, which should be accomplished by 2030.

While the increase in the base pension benefit is determined by the central government, the MOHRSS leaves room for discretion in extra pension benefits among different provinces. Table 2.1 provides the historical increase rates as stipulated by the MOHRSS, but these are just the suggested upper limits of the annual increase in the base pension benefit. Each province has its own discretion to raise the basic pension benefit up to the national upper limit by using a combination of fixed-amount, indexed, and preferential adjustment. According to the official announcement of the MOHRSS, the fixed-amount adjustment, a lump sum monthly payment that applies to every qualified benefit recipient, should reflect the principle of fairness.[11] In comparison, the indexed adjustment should incorporate incentives for larger and longer contribution by linking the increase to the years of contribution and the base pension amount. Additionally, the preferential adjustment should target specific disadvantaged groups of plan participants including veterans, old-age retirees, retirees living in remote and impoverished areas, and so forth. In Guangdong, the fixed-amount adjustments from 2016 to 2022 were CNY 35,

55, 50, 60, 60, 45, and 28 per month, respectively. For the same period, the indexed adjustments were 4.8%, 3.2%, 2.2%, 2.2%, 2.2%, 1.8%, and 2.1% of the base pension amount in the previous year. Moreover, there is usually some additional increase for more years of contribution and for disadvantaged members. In 2022, for example, the province offered extra CNY 1 per month for one more year of contribution (minimum CNY 15), and participants over 70, 80, 90, and 100 years will receive CNY 20, 30, 60, and 100 more per month in their base pension. When all three types of increase are considered, the mean aggregate annual increase rates roughly matched those stipulated by the MOHRSS, but the participants with larger pension bases and longer years of contribution and disadvantaged members were favored over other members. The funds needed for the annual increase will come from the social pool, but the prefecture and county governments may need to provide subsidies from their own budgets if there is a funding gap.

Along with Shandong, Guangdong was one of the first two provinces in China to invest its basic pension fund in financial markets. As early as 2012, Guangdong entrusted CNY 100 billion of its outstanding balance to the NCSSF for a period of five years. In 2017, the NCSSF returned the entrusted fund to Guangdong and the annualized investment return was about 8%.[12] In 2018 and 2019, Guangdong again sent a total of CNY 203 billion to the NCSSF for investment, ranking the first in the nation. However, compared to the total outstanding balance of the province, the total amount designated for investment has remained quite small. For instance, the accumulated balance in the basic pension fund reached CNY 1,233.8 billion in 2020 (Table 3.1), more than six times the total amount entrusted to the NCSSF. In recent years, there has been a call for the province to increase the level of investment to improve the overall return of the basic pension fund and of the enterprise and occupational annuity. Guangdong responded to that call by increasing the total entrusted investment of the basic pension, enterprise annuity, and occupational annuity to CNY 313.0 billion, 108.8 billion, and 182.9 billion, respectively. Moreover, there is also a demand for the pension fund to diversify its investment portfolio and to make more investments within the province. However, as it is strictly regulated by the "Measures on the Investment of Basic Pension Fund" issued by the State Council in 2015, Guangdong has not been able to make such changes in the management and investment practices of its pension fund.[13]

Finally, as in other provinces, the pension plan for public-sector employees of Guangdong was merged with the plan for enterprise workers in 2015.[14] Since January 1, 2016, just like other participants of the pension plan for enterprise workers, all public employees in the province have been required to contribute 8% of their wages to the individual account and another 4% to their occupational annuity. According to the Guangdong Statistical Yearbooks, the total participants of the pension plan for enterprise workers for the years 2013 to 2016 were 41.8, 48.1, 75.9, and 79.4 million, respectively, implying that the total number of public-sector participants (including working and retired public employees, teachers, doctors, etc.) who joined the plan in 2015 was probably between 20 and 25 million. To ensure a smooth transition from the previous system, the province made differentiated policies for "old persons" (who reached the retirement age on October 1, 2014, with less than 15 years of contribution), "middle persons" (hired before October 1, 2014, and expected to retire after that date), and "new persons" (hired on or after October 1, 2014). While the old pension policy applies to the old persons, the new pension policy only applies to the new persons. For the middle persons, a transition period of ten years was set up to guarantee that new retirees would receive at least the same level of benefits as they would have received before the merger of the two plans. During this period, a middle-person retiree's benefit remains the same as before if his/her benefit ends up being lower under the new policy. By contrast, if a middle-person retiree's benefit is higher under the new policy, he/she will only receive 10% of the additional amount if he/she retires in the first year (2015), then 20% if he/she retires in the second year (2016), and so on until 100% in the tenth year (2024). Although the basic pension funds for enterprise workers and public employees have been virtually the same since the merger in 2015, the two funds are managed separately in two special accounts pertaining to the HRSS of Guangdong. Due to its mandatory nature, the occupational annuity fund in Guangdong has been growing very fast since its inception. By the end of 2021, the total balance of this fund was CNY 182.9 billion. In comparison, the total balance of the enterprise annuity fund was only CNY 108.8 billion despite more years of accumulation.[15]

3.2.2 *Urban and rural residents' pension plan*

In 2019, Guangdong province issued a revised "Measures on the Implementation of the Urban and Rural Residents Pension Plan of Guangdong Province" that went into effect on January 1, 2020.[16] The "Measures" updated and replaced the old document issued in 2014, and they elaborated on many aspects of financing, benefits, governance, and other related areas of the management of this plan in the province.

As in other parts of the country, this plan covers anyone over 16 with a Guangdong Hukou who is not included in the two pension plans for urban enterprise workers and public-sector employees, excluding school students. Residents of Hongkong, Macao, and Taiwan are not included in this plan either and are subject to other specific regulations promulgated by the central government. From 2016 to 2021, the total enrollment of this plan gradually increased from 25.43 to 26.8 million (Table 3.3).[17] Qualified residents can participate in this plan at the place of their household registration on a voluntary basis. However, they must set up individual accounts to be able to

Table 3.3 Enrollment and Finance of Basic Pension Plan for Urban and Rural Residents in Guangdong

Year	Total Participants (Million)	Benefit Recipients (Million)	Total Revenue (Billion)	Total Expenditure (Billion)	Accumulated Balance (Billion)
2016	25.43	8.93	18.48	15.71	38.52
2017	25.87	9.58	18.80	17.10	40.30
2018	26.56	10.15	21.58	20.19	41.67
2019	26.42				
2020	26.57	9.05	28.31	26.53	47.51
2021	26.80	8.94	30.50	27.40	50.60

participate in this residents' pension plan. As stated in the "Measures", the basic principle of the urban and rural residents' pension plan is to "ensure the basic old-age needs, cover broad population, and be flexible and sustainable". In the meantime, by incorporating the government's effort with voluntary participation of the residents, this plan should set a benefit level that is consistent with the general level of economic and social development of the province and establish a management system that is compatible with the basic pension plan for urban enterprise workers and public-sector employees, along with other social welfare programs.

As described in the previous chapter, there are two main funding sources for the urban and rural residents' pension plan. The first funding source is government taxes at various levels to fund the base pension. Typically, this source constitutes the largest portion of revenue for this plan. For example, in 2016, CNY 14.07 billion out of the total revenue (CNY 18.48 billion) came from government taxes.[18] The second source is the annual contributions that plan participants pay to their mandatory individual accounts and the corresponding government subsidy. According to the current standards, there are nine levels of annual contribution for the province, and they are CNY 180, 240, 360, 600, 900, 1,200, 1,800, 3,600, and 4,800. The disabled, people living under the poverty line, and other groups in extreme difficulty can choose to contribute only CNY 120 a year. Plan participants can choose any of these nine levels to contribute for any one particular year. The social pool for urban and rural residents pension plan is subsidized by the government. The "Measures" stipulates that for those participants who choose to pay CNY 180, 240, and 360 annually, the government subsidy should be no less than CNY 30 per person (Table 3.4). For those who choose higher levels of contribution (CNY 600 or higher), the government subsidy should be no less than CNY 60 per person. For the 12 prefecture-level cities in the eastern (Shantou, Shanwei, Chaozhou, and Jieyang), western (Zhanjiang, Maoming, and Yangjiang), and northern regions (Shaoguan, Heyuan, Yunfu, Qingyuan, and Meizhou) of Guangdong, and Huizhou, Zhaoqing, and three municipalities of Jiangmen (Enping,

Table 3.4 Typical Contribution and Benefit Levels for the Urban and Rural Resident Pension Plan in Guangdong, 2022 (Unit: CNY)

Individual Contribution	Government Subsidy	Annual Withdrawal from Individual Account for 15 Years of Contribution[19]	Current Annual Base Pension[20]	Total Benefit
180	30	272	2,280	2,552
240	30	350	2,280	2,630
360	30	505	2,280	2,785
600	60	855	2,280	3,135
900	60	1,243	2,280	3,523
1,200	60	1,632	2,280	3,912
1,800	60	2,409	2,280	4,689
3,600	60	4,740	2,280	7,020
4,800	60	6,294	2,280	8,574

Taishan, and Kaiping), the burden to finance above minimum subsidies is equally shared by the provincial, prefecture, and county governments. For other prefecture-level cities of the province (mostly located in the Pearl River Delta area and, therefore, richer), the financing burden is shared between corresponding prefecture and county governments. For people with economic difficulties, the prefecture and county governments should pay a minimum of CNY 120 plus a CNY 30 subsidy for each participant. The "Measures" also encourages governments with more financial ability and social forces to subsidize or donate more to the social pool of the urban and rural residents' pension plan, but this is not mandatory. All individual contributions, subsidies, and other revenues are designated to the participants' individual accounts, which are inheritable. The interest on the individual account balance is set by the provincial government. Finally, tax agencies at different levels are responsible for collecting individual contributions for this plan.

The pension benefits for the participants of the urban and rural residents' pension plan comes from two accounts: the base pension plan account and the individual account. Typically, any participant of this plan in Guangdong province can receive benefits from these two accounts for his/her lifetime, if he/she reaches the age of 60 and has contributed to the individual account for at least 15 years. Participants who are 60 or older but have not yet made 15 years of contribution can continue to contribute to their individual accounts until 65 with the same level of government subsidy. Those who are 65 or older but still have not made 15 years of contribution are allowed to make a one-time payment to make up for the required 15 years of contribution to be able to receive the base benefits, but the lump sum payment does not qualify for government subsidy. Plan participants who are over 60, but have not contributed for

15 years and do not wish to pay the one-time contribution, can withdraw the funding from their individual accounts, either in a lump sum or on a monthly basis, upon the participant's written request. Table 3.4 shows the typical plan benefit in 2022 from the base pension and individual account corresponding to the nine levels of annual contribution. For those who contribute for more than 15 years, the benefit from the base pension will be CNY 3/month higher for each additional year of contribution. In addition, the base pension benefit is adjusted every year by the provincial government according to the changes in average wage, inflation, and other social security standards. In any event, considering that the average wage (non-private sector) of Guangdong province in 2021 was over CNY 118,000, the benefit level for the urban and rural residents' pension plan is, as mentioned in the previous chapter, very low.

The funding burden for the base pension is shared by the provincial and prefecture governments, but the proportion of burden varies according to the financial capacity of the latter. Currently, the province is divided into four regions to share the burden of the base pension. For the poorest region, including most prefectures, counties, and districts of Shantou, Shaoguan, Heyuan, Meizhou, Huizhou, Shanwei, Qingyuan, Chaozhou, and Jieyang, the province is 100% responsible for the expenditure of the base pension. For the second region, which includes the 12 prefectures in the western and eastern areas, the provincial government is 85% responsible for the funding. For the third region, which encompasses the less developed prefectures, counties, or districts in the Pearl River Delta, the provincial government is 65% responsible for the spending. For the wealthiest region of the province, including Guangzhou, Shenzhen (which directly receives funds from the central government), Zhuhai, Foshan, Dongguan, Zhongshan, and Jiangmen, the prefecture and county governments are 100% responsible for funding the plan. What is more, prefecture or county governments are also 100% responsible for paying for extra costs due to higher local benefit standards, payment of the benefit of individual accounts in excess of 139 months, additional monthly payments to participants who have contributed for more than 15 years, and higher base pension benefits for old-age participants (usually over 65 years). (For example, in Yunfu, participants between 65 and 75 years will receive an extra CNY 2 per month, participants between 75 and 85 years will receive an extra CNY 5 per month, and participants over 85 will receive an extra CNY 8 per month.)[21]

There are notable variations among the 21 prefecture-level cities in contribution subsidies, base pension benefits, increases in subsidy or benefit, cost-of-living adjustments, etc. Table 3.5 offers a comparison of some representative cities in the four regions. It is obvious that the generosity of pension subsidy and benefit largely depends on the economic prosperity and financial ability of the administering city. For example, Guangzhou and Shenzhen, located in the Pearl River Delta region, provide the most generous subsidy and highest benefit level for the participants of this plan, whereas most other cities in the eastern, western, and northern Guangdong only offer the minimum level

Table 3.5 Comparison of Base Pension Contribution Subsidy and Benefit of Prefecture-Level Cities in Guangdong (Unit: CNY)

Prefecture-Level City	Contribution Subsidy	Base Pension Benefit	Additional Benefit for Longer Contribution	Extra Benefit for Old Age
Jieyang	Provincial level	Provincial level (190/month)	3/month for each additional year of contribution	N/A
Chaozhou	Provincial level	Provincial level (190/month)	3/month for each additional year of contribution	N/A
Maoming	Provincial level	Provincial level (190/month)	3/month for each additional year of contribution	N/A
Zhanjiang	Provincial level	Provincial level (190/month)	3/month for each additional year of contribution; 1%, 2%, 3%, 4%, 5%, 6% increase in the base pension per month for accumulated contribution over 10,000, 15,000, 20,000, 25,000, 35,000, and 50,000, respectively	N/A
Yunfu	Provincial level	Provincial level (190/month)	5/month for each additional year of contribution	2/month for 65–75 years; 5/month for 75–85 years; 8/month for over 85 years
Shaoguan	Provincial level	Provincial level (190/month)	3/month for each additional year of contribution	≥ 3/month for over 65 years
Guangzhou	360→420 600→600 900→780 1,200→870 1,800→960 3,600→960 4,800→960	237/month	6/month for each additional year of contribution	N/A
Shenzhen	180→30 240→40 360→50 600→70 900→80 1,200→90 1,800→100 3,600→120 4,800→150	483/month (322/month for those holding Shenzhen Hukous for less than eight years)	3/month for each additional year of contribution	50/month for 65–80 years; 100/month for over 80 years

of subsidy and benefit, as required by the provincial government. Although the benefits for longer years of contribution, old age, etc., also vary from city to city, the overall differences are quite small.

3.3   Heilongjiang: An economically stagnant province with net outflow of labor force

Heilongjiang is one of the three provinces in Northeast China (the other two are Jilin and Liaoning). Located in the northernmost and easternmost part of the country, Heilongjiang has 12 prefecture-level cities and one prefecture. In 2021, the total resident population of the province was 31.25 million, decreasing from 38.33 million in 2010, and the total GDP was CNY 1,487.9 billion, increasing from 1,036.86 million in 2010. Among China's provincial-level administrative divisions, Heilongjiang is the sixth largest by total area and the 15th most populous, but the second poorest by GDP per capita, or the third poorest by average wage per capita (see Figure 3.1). In most years during the last two decades, the GDP growth rate of Heilongjiang also underperformed. For instance, its nominal GDP grew by 6.1% from 2020 to 2021, while the national average for that period was 8.1%.[22]

There are two main reasons for the relatively small economic size and slow growth rate of Heilongjiang province. The first is the so-called rust belt problem resulting from the overly concentrated economic structure. As a part of Northeast China, Heilongjiang is China's traditional industrial base featuring a preponderance of heavy industry and a large stock of SOEs. However, since a big wave of privatization led to the closure of uncompetitive state-owned factories in the 1990s, the province has suffered a prolonged period of economic stagnation due to its failure to revitalize the local economy. The second reason is the shrinking and quickly ageing population of the province. From 2010 to 2021, the natural population growth rate rapidly declined from 2.32‰ to -5.11‰, leading to a net decline of 7.08 million in resident population. In the meantime, the percentage of old people (65 years or older) in the province steadily climbed from 8.32% in 2010 to 16.8% in 2021, exceeding the national average by about 2 percentage points. The ageing problem is worsened by a continuous outflow of the younger generation to other regions of the country, especially the coastal and southern provinces. According to the Heilongjiang Bureau of Statistics, the average net outflow of population was 126 thousand per year between 2000 and 2010 and 69.2 thousand per year between 2011 and 2015.[23] Most of the migrants from the province were people of working age between 30 and 39.

For Heilongjiang, the enduring economic stagnation and severely ageing population constitute a vicious circle, putting an enormous financial pressure on the pension system. On the one hand, the underperforming economy has led to a downturn in government revenue. In Fiscal Year 2020, revenue in the provincial government's general budget decreased by 8.7%. On the other hand, the large and increasing percentage of old-age population demanded more public spending on social welfare programs. In 2020, the general expenditure of the province increased by 8.7%, and 87% of the total budget was spent on social welfare. As a result, Heilongjiang has become one of the provinces with the lowest dependency ratio (< 1.3) and the worst pension deficit in the nation since the early 2010s (refer to Table 2.10 and Table 2.11).

3.3.1 Basic pension plans for urban enterprise workers and public-sector employees

Since 2016, despite a significant decline in the total resident population of the province, the total enrollment in the basic pension plan for urban enterprise workers and public-sector employees in Heilongjiang grew steadily from 11.44 million to 14.47 million (see Table 3.6). However, as the ageing problem became severe in the province, the total number of retirees grew at a faster rate than that of workers contributing to the two pension plans, leading to a rapidly decreasing dependency ratio over the same period. For example, the dependency ratio was 1.34 in 2016, the lowest among all provincial governments, whereas the national average was 2.8 for the same year. Since the early 2010s, Heilongjiang has been suffering from large annual deficits in its basic pension plans, and this has in turn caused a large negative accumulated balance, which is one of the worst among provincial governments in the nation. According to the "China Social Insurance Annual Development Report 2016", the total pension fund balance of Heilongjiang could pay for less than one month of its ongoing pension obligations while that of Guangdong could pay for more than 55 months.

To deal with the severe pension deficit, both the central government of China and the provincial government have taken several major measures. At the central level, the first measure was to increase intergovernmental transfers to help the province to ensure timely payment of pension benefits. For instance, the central government transferred a total of CNY 267.4 billion to the province in 2016, about 20% of which was used to pay for pension benefits.[26] The second was to implement a national coordination mechanism, which is designed to transfer part of the pension surpluses of some provinces (e.g., Guangdong) to the provinces with severe pension deficits. As Table 3.6 shows, Heilongjiang has been receiving a significant amount of subsidies from the national coordination mechanism since 2018. At the provincial level, the Heilongjiang government has routinely used its budgetary revenues to support the pension system. In 2016, the province spent CNY 73.24 billion on social security and insurance programs, and that number increased to CNY 132.99 billion in 2021. Another important measure at the provincial level was to transfer part of the state-owned capital to replenish its depleted pension

Table 3.6 Enrollment and Finance of Basic Pension Plan for Urban Enterprise Workers and Public-Sector Employees in Heilongjiang

Year	Total Members (Million)	Contributing Workers (Million)	Retirees (Million)	Dependency Ratio	Total Revenue (Billion)	Total Expenditure (Billion)	Accumulated Balance (Billion)	Net Subsidy (Billion)
2016	11.44	6.56	4.89	1.34	100.57	133.27	−19.61	
2017	12.06	6.82	5.24	1.30	124.05	153.42	−48.62	
2018	13.09	7.32	5.77	1.27	163.02	179.31	−55.72	9.19
2019	13.65	7.65	6.00	1.28	178.54	209.48	−43.37	43.30
2020	14.11	7.90	6.21	1.27	162.93	224.01	−36.89	48.56
2021	14.47	8.12	6.35	1.28	182.45	245.68	−37.23	54.70
2022	15.07	8.51	6.56	1.30	185.18	249.29	−10.21	82.16

Sources: The HRSS of Heilongjiang Annual Bulletin[24]; Heilongjiang Bureau of Statistics.[25]

fund. According to the current plan, all eligible state-owned enterprises in the province should transfer 10% of their total equity as assessed on November 10, 2017.[27] As a result of all these efforts, the pension fund balance has somewhat improved in the past three years, but the overall situation of the two basic pension plans has not fundamentally changed due to the many underlying economic and demographic problems.

Heilongjiang was one of first provinces in China to achieve the goal of pooling the funds for the basic pension plan for urban enterprise workers and public-sector employees at the provincial level. As early as in 2013, the province had taken steps to centralize the pension contribution, benefit, and governance at the provincial level. For example, the contribution rate for enterprises was lowered from about 25.4% to 22% for most prefecture-level cities (20% for Daqing and Suifenhe), and the contribution rate for employees was set at 8% for all cities. Around 2018, the province begun to use a single average wage to calculate the contribution and benefits for the entire province. Since January 1, 2020, the province has formally unified all important aspects of its pension plan, including the enrollment criteria, base and percentage for the contribution, calculation of the benefit, governance, budgeting, and distribution of financial burden.[28] The details of all these aspects are consistent with the policies promulgated by the central government. Every year before the end of October, the HRSS of the province issues a "full-caliber" social average wage to be used for pension purposes for the next year. From 2018 to 2023, the provincial-level social average wages were CNY 4,645/month, 4,735/month, 4,835/month, 5,120/month, 5,865/month, and 6,430/month, respectively. However, a quick glimpse at city-level average wages also reveals a great discrepancy among the 12 prefectures. For instance, in 2020, the highest annual wage in the province was CNY 96,088 (Daqing), whereas the lowest was only CNY 50,319 (Yichun). What then made it possible for the province to adopt a unified base for its pension plans so promptly? A possible reason is that the majority of urban workers in the province are largely concentrated in just a few big cities, such as Harbin and Qiqihar. In 2020, for example, the total population of these two cities accounted for almost half the 32 million population of the province. Since the difference in wages among the few large cities in Heilongjiang was not dramatic, adopting a unified provincial-level wage base for the social pooling would not cause serious problems.

Although the formula for calculating the retirement benefit for the two pension plans is the same in Heilongjiang, the annual increase in the retirement benefit appears to be more generous in that province than in other provinces. From 2018 to 2020, the annual rates of increase announced by the MOHRSS and the MOF were 5.0%, 5.0%, and 5.0%, but Heilongjiang raised the rates to 6.0%, 5.5%, and 5.5% using a combination of fixed-amount, indexed, and preferential adjustments.[29] When summarizing the lessons and challenges of implementing provincial-level social pooling, one official document of the

HRSS of the province explained the rationale behind this more generous increase in pension benefit as follows:[30]

> Although the basic pension level of enterprise retirees has been improved in recent years, the problem of low level is still very prominent. After eight consecutive years of adjusting the basic pension of enterprise retirees, the per-capita basic pension level of urban enterprise retirees in our province has been greatly improved, but the basic pension level is still relatively low compared with other provinces and cities in China, and it is very mismatched with the per capita GDP and salary level of our province. The reasons for this phenomenon are not only related to the implementation of the basic pension insurance system, but also to the unsoundness of the adjustment mechanism for the basic pension. Therefore, we suggest that the central government, in adjusting the basic pension of retired employees, should give the province a certain degree of flexibility under the overall policy framework formulated by the state, so as to develop a scientific and reasonable adjustment mechanism in accordance with the actual situation and the characteristics of our province.

Based on the above rationale, Heilongjiang has also been implementing a more generous adjustment mechanism for the basic pension plans. From 2011 to 2015, the average benefit level for retirees almost doubled from CNY 1,076/month to 2,119/month. Although the annual increase rate has remained the same as the national rate in recent years, the accumulated growth in the benefit level has been considerable over the last decade. As a result, the average benefit level in Heilongjiang is comparable with that of most other provinces, despite significantly lower average wages and dependency ratios. In 2015, the average monthly wage for enterprise workers in Guangdong was CNY 5,525, with a replacement ratio of 0.43, whereas the average monthly wage for enterprise workers in Heilongjiang was CNY 4,073 but with a replacement ratio of 0.52.[31] As such, the resulting benefit level for enterprise retirees was almost identical for the two provinces. In addition, there are also many so-called five-seven workers or dependent workers in the province because the province used to be the center of heavy industries in China in the 1960s and 1970s. These people, usually family members of enterprise workers, worked in state-owned enterprises (typically petroleum, coal, chemical, or other heavy industries) as temporary employees who should have been but actually were not covered by any pension plans. From 2004 to 2011, about 550,000 five-seven workers, 250,000 dependent workers, and 170,000 other workers of similar nature were allowed to participate in the basic pension plan for urban enterprise workers. Therefore, as the province has taken steps to solve the pension problem of these people by including them in the basic pension plan with substantial government subsidies, the financial burden for the pension system has become even heavier in recent years, making it harder for the province to balance the income and expenditure of its basic pension plan.

According to the "Pilot Implementation Program to Improve Urban Social Security System of Heilongjiang Province",[32] the funds in the social pool and in the individual account should be managed separately, and the individual account fund should be managed by the provincial social insurance agency and incorporated into the special financial account of the social security fund. In accordance with national regulations, the provincial government should develop detailed measures to guide and supervise fund management and investment operations. While the central financial assistance is usually entrusted by the province to the NCSSF to invest and commit to a certain rate of return, subsidies from provincial financial resources are invested and operated by the province in accordance with national regulations, and the provincial government is responsible for preserving and increasing the value of the fund.[33] As described earlier (see Table 3.6), Heilongjiang has been accumulating a large pension deficit since early 2010s, and the province is heavily relying on financial subsidies from both central and subnational governments to pay for pension obligations. Therefore, it is not surprising that the province has little extra funds to engage in investment activities, although it did sign an entrustment agreement with the NSSF for a short period. In 2015, with the approval of both the MOF and the MOHRSS, Heilongjiang disbursed the entrusted principal and interests totaling CNY 15 billion and dissolved the entrusted investment management relationship with the NSSF.[34]

3.3.2 Urban and rural residents' pension plan

Heilongjiang launched its first pilot program for its new rural pension plan in late 2009 and a pilot program for an urban residents' pension plan in 2011. By July 2013, the two plans covered more than 7.95 million residents, with a participation rate of 86.7% for people aged 60 or older. In February 2014, according to the mandate of the State Council, the two pension plans were merged into one unified rural and urban residents' pension plan, which has grown steadily in both number of participants and accumulated balance since then. As Table 3.7 shows, the total enrollment of the unified plan increased from 8.38 to 9.17 million from 2016 to 2019, covering almost every qualified rural and urban resident in the province.[35] This number fell slightly to 8.90 million from 2020 to 2022, most likely due to the shrinking population in the rural areas of the province. From 2018 to 2022, the total revenue was always greater than the total expenditure of the plan, leading to a total of CNY 15.23 billion accumulated balance by the end of 2022. Typically, the revenue for this plan comes from two sources: premiums collected from individual participants and subsidies from the central, provincial, and local governments. In 2013, for instance, the total premiums collected in the province amounted

Table 3.7 Enrollment and Finance of Basic Pension Plan for Urban and Rural Residents in Heilongjiang

Year	Total Members (Million)	Urban Residents (Million)	Rural Residents (Million)	Benefit Recipients (Million)	Total Revenue (Billion)	Total Expenditure (Billion)	Accumulated Balance (Billion)
2016	8.38			3.10			
2017	8.40			3.28			
2018	8.97	0.47	8.50	3.48	5.30	4.25	8.06
2019	9.17	0.49	8.68	3.61	6.49	4.62	9.96
2020	9.09	0.48	8.60	3.67	6.32	4.66	11.63
2021	8.90	0.49	8.42	3.62	6.86	4.82	13.67
2022	8.90	0.50	8.40	3.68	6.50	4.94	15.23

Table 3.8 Typical Annual Contribution and Benefit Levels for the Urban and Rural Resident Pension Plan in Heilongjiang, 2022 (Unit: CNY)

Individual Contribution	Government Subsidy	Annual Withdrawal from Individual Account for 15 years of Contribution	Current Annual Base Pension[36]	Total Annual Benefit
200	40	311	1,416	1,727
300	50	453	1,416	1,869
400	60	596	1,416	2,012
500	70	738	1,416	2,154
600	70	868	1,416	2,284
700	70	997	1,416	2,413
800	70	1,127	1,416	2,543
900	70	1,256	1,416	2,672
1,000	70	1,386	1,416	2,802
1,500	100	2,072	1,416	3,488
2,000	120	2,745	1,416	4,161
3,000	140	4,066	1,416	5,482

to CNY 2.23 billion, while the central government transferred a total of CNY 1.18 billion to the province and the provincial and local governments matched the subsidies with CNY 0.72 billion.

In 2013, the base pension benefit for the urban and rural residents' plan in most areas of the province was CNY 55 per person per month, which was lower than the national average of CNY 78.6 per person per month. However, the base pension benefit was raised to CNY 80 per person per month in 2017 and then raised again to CNY 118 per person per month in 2022. Table 3.8 shows the typical annual contribution and benefit levels for this plan. If a plan participant contributes the minimum level for 15 years, he/

she will receive CNY 1,727 per year, or CNY 144 per month after the age of 60. Although this represents a 114% increase from the level of 2013, the benefit level of the urban and rural residents' plan in Heilongjiang remains below the national average, which was CNY 179 per person per month in 2022. In addition, the overall expenditure per person for this plan, which can be calculated by dividing the total expenditure by the total number of benefit recipients, reveals that the vast majority of the participants of this plan only contribute the minimum of the required annual level to the plan's individual account to take advantage of the government subsidies. For example, the average annual benefit in 2021 was about CNY 1,331 per person, which was just a little higher than the minimum benefit level for the same year (CNY 1,271). While this may be a national phenomenon, it is particularly so in Heilongjiang, where most of the participants of this plan are probably rural residents.

Because of the relatively low level of pension benefit, stable number of plan participants, and large government subsidy, the overall financial condition of the urban and rural pension plan of Heilongjiang has remained relatively healthy in recent years. As reported in Table 3.7, the accumulated total balance of the plan has climbed steadily, from CNY 8.06 billion to 15.13 billion between 2018 and 2022. This achievement is particularly noteworthy considering that the overall financial and pension environment of the province is probably the worst in the country. Given that the plan has sufficient reserves to pay for ongoing pension obligations, in 2018, Heilongjiang issued the "Opinions on the Determination of the Benefit Level of Urban and Rural Residents' Pension Plan and the Establishment of Normal Adjustment Mechanism of the Basic Pension"[37] to raise the pension benefit level gradually. According to these "Opinions", the provincial government should, by taking account of the province's economic development and income growth, establish a normal adjustment mechanism for the minimum base pension benefit level for urban and rural residents. As a consequence of this policy, the province has not only raised the base pension level twice by about 20% for all plan participants since 2014 but also increased the pension benefits for elderly and disadvantaged participants. For instance, retirees aged 65 to 79 are qualified to receive an extra CNY 5 per month, and retirees 80 or over receive an extra CNY 10 per month. In addition, Heilongjiang has waived pension contributions for all participants who live in poverty, totaling about 0.48 million urban and rural residents in 2022.[38]

In contrast to the basic pension plan of the province, the urban and rural resident plan has signed an entrustment agreement with the NSSF and invested 100% of its new fund balance every year. By the end of 2022, the total entrusted investment fund of the province reached 7.65 billion.[39] The successful investment of the account balance has helped the plan to preserve its fund value as well as to improve its benefit level.

3.4   Sichuan: An inland province with stable economic growth and large labor force

Sichuan is an inland and mountainous province in Southwest China, occupying the easternmost part of the Tibetan Plateau on the west, the Daba Mountains in the north, and the Yungui Plateau to the south. The province has a total area of 485,000 square kilometers, ranking 5th in the country, and it is currently divided into 21 prefecture-level divisions. In antiquity, Sichuan was the home to the ancient state of Ba and the kingdom of Shu during the Three Kingdoms era (220–280 AD), but it has remained remote from the political centers throughout the history of China. Although Sichuan traditionally has been an area of multiple ethnic minorities including Yi, Tibetan, and Qiang, today, the Han ethnicity is the province's largest ethnic group, making up about 95% of the total population.

The GDP of Sichuan reached CNY 5,675 billion ($822 billion) in 2022, ranking 6th in the nation or 18th in the world if it is compared to a country. Historically known as the Province of Abundance, Sichuan is one of China's main agricultural centers producing grain, rice, pork, sugarcane, and various other commercial crops. Sichuan is also rich in mineral reserves, such as iron, petroleum, natural gas, vanadium, titanium, etc. Benefiting greatly from these natural resources, Sichuan has developed into one of the major industrial centers of China, comprising such heavy industries as coal, energy, and steel, and such light industries as building materials, wood, food, silk, and textiles. In the last two decades, the province has made great strides to develop modern high-tech industries by encouraging domestic and foreign investments, and today's Sichuan has grown into an important industrial base for electronics and information technology, hydropower, auto, aerospace and defense, and so forth. In addition to agriculture and industry, Sichuan's beautiful landscape and rich historical relics have also made the province an attraction for tourism. Overall, a striking feature the economy of Sichuan is its well-diversified and balanced economic structure, which helps the province to maintain stable and relatively high economic growth rates. Before the pandemic of 2019, the average annual GDP growth rate for Sichuan was above 8%; from 2020 to 2022, despite the great impact of the pandemic, Sichuan still managed to achieve positive growth rates of 3.8%, 8.2%, and 2.9%, respectively, which were among the highest in the country during this three-year period.[40]

As the 5th-most populous province in the nation, Sichuan has a population of 83.68 million according to the latest national census data of 2020. Before Chongqing Municipality was separated from the province in 1997, the province had remained China's most populous province since its establishment in 1955. Traditionally, Sichuan is known as a large supplier of labor to other regions of the country, especially to the Pearl River Delta and the Yangtse River Delta.[41] In 2020, the total number of outgoing workers from the province was 10.4 million, 25.3% of whom went to Guangdong province, and

19.1% went to Zhejiang and Jiangsu provinces.[42] However, as the Sichuan-Chongqing metropolitan area gathers momentum for economic growth, an increasing percentage of workers from smaller cities or rural areas of Sichuan is choosing to stay in its capital city, Chengdu, or go to the nearby city, Chongqing. In 2020, the resident population of Chengdu exceeded 20 million for the first time and about 10.9% of the outflowing population chose Chongqing as their destination.[43] Over the past decade, the trend towards urbanization has accelerated in Sichuan, and the urbanization rate has grown from 40.2% in 2010 to 56.7% in 2020. For the same time period, the proportion of old people over 60 has also climbed from 16.3% to 21.7% of its total population.

The economic and demographic features of Sichuan have brought about two potential challenges for the pension system of the province. First, while Sichuan's economy is well diversified and fast growing, the province has always had difficulties in attracting young workers from other regions of the country, partly because of its remoteness and less convenient transportation. As the current labor force in the province is ageing, its pension plan for enterprise workers will experience higher pressure. However, this problem may be partly mitigated by the slowing outflow of labor to other provinces. In addition, Sichuan is a higher education center with 134 universities and more than 2 million enrolled college students. This may also help the provincial government to recruit more young talents in the near future if it produces adequate talent policies. Second, for historical reasons, Sichuan is home to a large population of migrant workers. When the early generations (starting in the 1980s) of these workers reach retirement age and come back to their hometowns, the basic pension plan for urban and rural residents in the province will be faced with enormous pressure to raise the benefit level because the current level, about CNY 100 per month for most participants, is far from enough to maintain a minimum living standard.

3.4.1 *Basic pension plans for urban enterprise workers and public-sector employees*

The Wenchuan earthquake in 2008 devastated the western part of Sichuan, causing 69.2 thousand deaths and direct economic losses of CNY 845 billion. However, the province swiftly recovered from the wound caused by the earthquake and gradually increased the pension coverage for urban enterprise workers in the subsequent years. As Table 3.9 shows, the number of total participants of the plan rose from 21.58 million to 31.79 million, about a 47.3% increase, from 2016 to 2021. For the same period, thanks to the accelerated urbanization and slowdown of labor outflow, the number of contributing workers rose by 59.5%, even faster than the number of total participants. As a result, despite the worsening ageing problem in the province, the basic pension plan of Sichuan has seen a slightly upward trend of dependency ratio,

Table 3.9 Enrollment and Finance of Basic Pension Plan for Urban Enterprise Workers and Public-Sector Employees in Sichuan

Year	Total Members (Million)	Contributing Workers (Million)	Retirees (Million)	Dependency Ratio	Total Revenue (Billion)	Central Subsidy (Billion)	Local Subsidy (Billion)	Total Expenditure (Billion)	Accumulated Balance (Billion)
2016	21.58	13.80	7.80	1.77	274.30	38.42	0.21	267.99	222.63
2017	23.35	15.19	8.16	1.86	329.30	44.10	17.59	227.64	324.58
2018	25.44	16.62	8.82	1.88	307.17	49.71	0.39	263.07	368.68
2019	27.00	17.85	9.16	1.95	309.38	55.67	0.17	302.12	375.95
2020	28.30	18.83	9.48	1.99	305.58	64.36	0.12	344.79	336.74
2021	31.79	22.01	9.77	2.25	330.30	62.44	0.39	293.25	358.85

climbing from 1.77 in 2016 to 2.25 in 2021. On the revenue side, Sichuan's basic pension plan has managed to maintain a healthy condition partly because the plan has absorbed more contributing members during the past few years and partly because the province has been receiving an increasing amount of subsidy from the central government. On the expenditure side, the province has not experienced dramatic changes in its benefit structure since 2016, so the total expenditure has grown mildly in tandem with the growth in the number of retirees. Except for 2020, when the province's pension basic pension plan recorded a large deficit of about CNY 40 billion, all other years during the period recorded fund surpluses, resulting in a climbing accumulated account balance in the range of CNY 320~375 billion. It should be noted that Sichuan has to rely on the transfer payments from the central government to maintain a positive pension account balance. Compared to central transfers, subsidies from local governments have been negligible in recent years.

Like Heilongjiang and many other provinces, Sichuan followed the order by the MOHRSS, the MOF, and the State Taxation Administration of the central government and issued the "Announcement about Standardizing the Implementation of the Provincial Coordination of the Sichuan Provincial Government's Enterprise Workers' Basic Pension Plan" (hereafter "the announcement") in 2020.[44] In this announcement, the province clearly laid out the goals, on the basis of the unification of income and expenditure at the municipal level, to standardize and unify pension policies, fund collection and expenditure management, budget management, responsibility-sharing mechanisms, information systems, etc., further at the provincial level, and it also specified policy means and a timeline to achieve those goals. Since there seems to be no dramatic disparity in average wage among different areas of Sichuan (Table 3.10), the province has largely achieved the goal of centralizing the basic pension by the end of 2021.[45] According to the HRSS of the province, the provincial-level, full-caliber social average wages to be used for pension purposes were CNY 6,210/month, 6,785/month, and 7,076/month for 2020 to 2022, respectively. In many aspects, the announcement outlined important legal, fiscal, and institutional frameworks for the basic pension plan of Sichuan.

The core mission of the announcement was to centralize the fund account and management of the basic pension plan at the provincial level under the principle of two lines of income and expenditure.[46] For the pension fund collection, beginning on December 1, 2020, the current pension premiums collected by tax departments at all levels were pooled into the provincial treasury, and the Department of Finance of the province then transferred the funds to a unified provincial social insurance financial account in accordance with the regulations of the central government. For the pension fund distribution, also beginning on December 1, 2020, the HRSS of Sichuan first reviewed and approved the expenditure requested by local governments on a monthly basis,

Table 3.10 Average Monthly Wage and Proportion of Financial Burden of Basic Pension Insurance for Enterprise Workers in Each Prefecture-Level City

Prefecture-Level City	Monthly Wage in 2021 (CNY)	Proportion of Burden
Chengdu	7,655	3.0%
Zigong	6,514	1.4%
Panzhihua	7,163	1.4%
Luzhou	6,002	1.7%
Deyang	6,406	1.4%
Mianyang	6,374	1.3%
Guangyuan	6,017	1.1%
Suining	5,387	1.3%
Neijiang	6,058	1.0%
Leshan	6,337	1.3%
Nanchong	6,673	1.1%
Yibin	6,320	1.5%
Guangan	5,516	1.3%
Dazhou	6,115	1.0%
Bazhong	5,644	1.3%
Yaan	5,939	1.2%
Meishan	6,269	1.5%
Ziyang	6,517	1.2%
Aba	9,015	1.2%
Ganzi	8,595	1.4%
Liangshan	7,412	1.4%

and upon the approval of the Department of Finance, the HRSS then allocated the approved amount to the fund accounts of local governments at all levels from the unified provincial social insurance account. In addition, the central transfers and financial subsidies were submitted to the provincial treasury account and included in the provincial integrated fund, which was uniformly managed, used, and dispatched by the provincial government. Expenditures made by localities in violation of the unified national and provincial policies were not included in the unified pension fund account of the province.

Another important mission of the announcement was to establish a formal responsibility-sharing mechanism between the province and the local governments. According to the "Measures for Sharing Responsibility for Provincial Coordination of Basic Pension Insurance for Enterprise Workers in Sichuan Province" issued together with the announcement,[47] the provincial government establishes a unified mechanism for sharing the responsibilities for the basic pension in the whole province under the principle of "unified revenue and expenditure, hierarchical responsibility structure, corresponding rights with responsibilities, and reasonable sharing among all governments", and it determines the responsibility for sharing the fund gap between the governments at all levels for the fund shortfalls to ensure timely and full payment in the province. In areas with general shortfalls in current pension fund revenue (the fund revenue is less than the fund expenditure in the current budget year), 70% of the current pension fund expenditures are borne by the provincial pooled fund; if 70% of the current expenditures is smaller than the current pension revenues, the provincial pooled fund will pay back the difference between the current revenues and 70% of the current expenditures to the local government and the remaining part should come from the local accumulated pension fund balance; and if the local accumulated balance is still insufficient to make up for the fund gap, 1%–3% of local government current fiscal revenues must be allocated to pay for the pension expenditures. Table 3.10 provides the specific burden ratio for each area, which may reflect the economic, demographic, and possibly some other considerations of the provincial government. In areas with no general shortfalls, 70% of current expenditures come from the provincial coordinated fund, and the remaining part comes from either the old local balance or the provincial fund if the former is insufficient. For areas with accumulated administrative shortfalls due to the violation of national and provincial unified policy, failure to complete the annual income plan, failure to expand the scope of expenditure or raise the standard of expenditure, and so forth, the local governments are fully responsible for the fund gaps. Finally, for areas with annual surpluses in the basic pension premium, the HRSS in conjunction with the Department of Finance of Sichuan will establish a separate account for the local government and reserve 50% of the surpluses to offset local general shortfalls for subsequent years.

The HRSS of Sichuan is one of the few that provide comprehensive and consistent information about the pensions of public-sector employees. Based on those data, Figure 3.3 reports the trend of total retirees and average annual

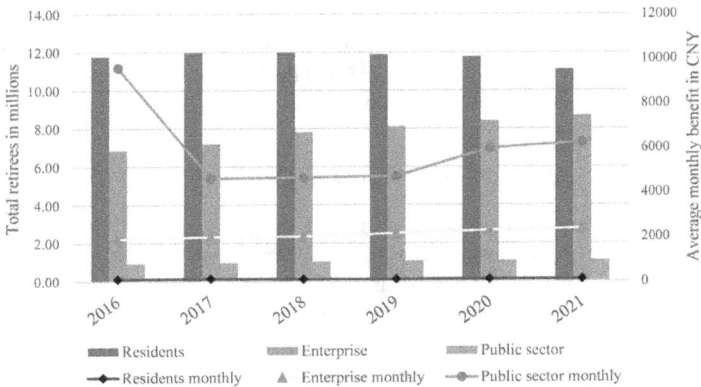

Figure 3.3 Total Members and Average Monthly Benefit for Urban and Rural Residents, Enterprise Workers, and Public-Sector Employees in Sichuan

retirement benefits for the urban and rural residents', urban enterprise workers', and the public-sector employees' pension plans from 2016 to 2021. During the period, the total number of retirees in the public sector grew slightly from 0.93 to 1.1 million, whereas the number of retirees participating in the basic pension plan for enterprise workers increased steadily from 6.85 to 8.67 million, and the number of beneficiaries participating in the urban and rural residents' plan fell slightly from 11.98 to 11.1 million. The trend in the public sector revealed that this sector did not grow much in size under a tight nationwide control over the recruitment of public employees, with the slight increase in retirees mostly reflecting the natural ageing of the members. In contrast, the significant increase in the retirees of the plan for urban enterprise workers partly resulted from the attractiveness of the benefit design of the plan and partly from the mandatory nature of the plan. Compared with the other two plans, the pension plan for urban and rural residents was the only one that saw a declining trend in total retirees, possibly due to the very low benefit level, which failed to attract continuous participation. With respect to average pension benefits, the three plans differed greatly in both absolute amount and growth trend. Among the three plans, the plan for public employees provided the highest average monthly benefit for its retirees. Since it was merged with the plan for urban enterprise workers in 2016 (the particularly high number for 2016 may reflect some transitional expenses), its average benefit was at least twice as much as that for urban enterprise workers, and it also grew more quickly than the latter. In 2021, the average monthly benefit for public-sector retirees reached CNY 6,242, almost three times as much as that for urban enterprise workers. In comparison, the average monthly benefit for enterprise workers grew slowly from CNY 1,886 to 2,364 during the same period, whereas that for the urban and rural residents' plan almost remained unchanged at a little over CNY 100. To a large extent, the detailed information contained in Figure 3.3 reflects some of the key differences in the pension benefit design, as well as the logic behind the pension policies in China.

3.4.2   *Urban and rural residents' pension plan*

Following the mandate of the State Council, the government of Sichuan combined its new rural pension plan and urban residents' pension plan, and it established a unified rural and urban residents' pension plan in 2014.[48] From 2016 to 2019, the total number of participants steadily climbed from 30.52 to 33.69 million, but it slowly declined to 31.81 million in the next two years. In 2020, for example, the aggregate number of participants in public pension plans reached 60.5 million, covering 72.35% of the total population of Sichuan. Although this is not consistent with the national trend (see Table 2.8), it is similar to Heilongjiang province. As reported in the 4th column of Table 3.11, the total revenue increased very fast from 2016 to 2021, especially in 2020

Table 3.11 Enrollment and Finance of Pension Plan for Urban and Rural Residents in Sichuan

Year	Total Members (Million)	Benefit Recipients (Million)	Total Revenue (Billion)	Central Subsidy (Billion)	Local Subsidy (Billions)	Total Expenditure (Billion)	Accumulated Balance (Billion)
2016	30.52	11.75	19.04	9.59	1.81	14.16	35.18
2017	30.75	11.98	25.02	9.91	2.11	15.98	44.22
2018	32.22	11.98	24.65	11.61	2.02	20.03	48.84
2019	33.69	11.88	24.67	11.45	2.83	20.40	53.11
2020	32.24	11.77	31.39	12.40	3.11	21.25	63.25
2021	31.81	11.10	38.41	13.02	3.36	23.10	78.56

and 2021. While the subsidies from both the central and local governments have also increased during the same period, the largest source of pension revenue growth has come from individual contributions. For instance, individual contributions increased by CNY 5.5 billion from 2019 to 2020, larger than the total increase in other categories combined for the same year. In contrast, the total number of benefit recipients did not change much or even decreased slightly after 2018. Therefore, despite the steady growth in per-capita pension benefit due to policy adjustment, the accumulated balance of this pension plan more than doubled from 2016 to 2021.

Sichuan established the basic design for the pension plan for urban and rural residents in the "Implementation Opinions on Establishing a Unified Basic Pension Insurance System for Urban and Rural Residents", promulgated in 2014,[49] which was later amended in 2020, and did not change dramatically thereafter except for minor improvements. This document stipulated 13 levels of individual contribution from CNY 100 to CNY 3,000 and the corresponding levels of government subsidy from CNY 40 to 160 (Table 3.12). Three more contribution levels, namely, CNY 4,000, 5,000, and 6,000, were added in 2020 and 2022 to allow plan participants to reap more government subsidies by contributing more to their individual accounts. As of 2023, the base annual pension benefit for Sichuan's urban and rural residents' plan has been raised to CNY 1,380 per year (or CNY 115 per month), higher than the national minimum standard of CNY 93 per month in 2020 but lower than that of most other provinces. Table 3.12 reports the 13 contribution levels, the corresponding government subsidy, and annual pension benefit for a typical plan participant. According to this table, if a participant contributes the minimum level for 15 years, he/she will receive CNY 1,691 per year, or about CNY 141 per month after the age of 60. Although this minimum benefit level is below the national average of CNY 179 per month in 2022, Sichuan allows for higher levels of contribution and provides more generous subsidies for participants contributing more to their individual accounts. As a result, participants in the urban and rural residents' plan in Sichuan may not be particularly

Table 3.12 Typical Annual Contribution and Benefit Levels for the Urban and Rural Resident Pension Plan in Sichuan, 2023[51] (Unit: CNY)

Individual Contribution	Government Subsidy	Annual Withdrawal from Individual Account for 15 Years of Contribution	Current Annual Base Pension	Total Annual Benefit
200	40	311	1,380	1,691
300	45	447	1,380	1,827
400	50	583	1,380	1,963
500	60	725	1,380	2,105
600	60	855	1,380	2,235
700	65	991	1,380	2,371
800	70	1,127	1,380	2,507
900	75	1,263	1,380	2,643
1,000	80	1,399	1,380	2,779
1,500	100	2,072	1,380	3,452
2,000	120	2,745	1,380	4,125
3,000	160	4,092	1,380	5,472
4,000	200	5,439	1,380	6,819
5,000	240	6,786	1,380	8,166
6,000	280	8,132	1,380	9,512

disadvantaged when compared to their counterparts in other provinces. The average pension expenditure for benefit recipients was CNY 2,081 per year (calculated from the 3rd and 7th column of Table 3.11), revealing that the participants took advantage of the design of this plan by contributing about CNY 500 on average or CNY 300 more than the minimum required amount to their individual accounts. For instance, if a plan member contributes CNY 500 per year for 15 years, he/she will receive CNY 2,105 per year after retirement, which is similar to the benefit level of Heilongjiang but still significantly lower than that of Guangdong. In recent years, the government of Sichuan has recognized this problem and has clearly stated that "to steadily increase the level of social insurance benefits" is one of the important goals of the "Fourteenth Five-Year Plan for the Development of Human Resources and Social Security in Sichuan Province".[50]

According to the "Implementation Opinion" of 2014, Sichuan's urban and rural residents' pension insurance fund should be incorporated into the financial account of the social security fund and managed on two lines of income and expenditure, with separate accounts and accounting. When the integration of the locally managed urban and rural residents' pension insurance system is completed, the province will gradually promote the provincial-level management of a unified urban and rural residents' pension fund. However, by the beginning of 2023, the province had only started the prefectural-level municipal coordination of the urban and rural residents' pension plan, and the provincial-level coordination had not yet been achieved. The "Implementation Opinion" also stipulated the investment principles: "the urban and rural residents' pension insurance fund will be invested and operated in accordance with the unified regulations of the State, so as to realize the preservation of value and increase in value". Therefore, the urban and rural residents' plan has also entrusted the investment of its fund balance to the NSSF. Although the HRSS of Sichuan does not release detailed information about the investment of each pension fund, the total entrusted investment fund, including the accumulated balance of both the basic pension plan for urban enterprise workers and public-sector employees, and the urban and rural residents' plan, reached CNY 100 and 123 billion in 2020 and 2021, respectively.[52]

3.5 Summary of the three cases

This chapter has compared the three pension plans in Guangdong, Heilongjiang, and Sichuan, providing a detailed account of the real pension situation in these provinces. At the current stage of development, there is an evident national trend towards a more centralized and unified pension system, and many important elements in pension design, including enrollment criteria, range of coverage, contribution rate, formulae for calculating benefits, management and investment regulations, etc., are almost identical in the three provinces. However, the transition towards a national pension system is not complete yet, and a significant number of noticeable differences remain among provinces in terms of pension coordination, benefit level, governance, adjustment schemes, investment practices, and so forth. By summarizing the three cases, we can learn the following lessons, which may hopefully enlighten the ongoing pension reforms in China.

As our analysis clearly reveals, China has been taking decisive measures to centralize the previously fragmented and locally administered pension plans quickly by establishing a unified pension system. Among the three provinces studied in this chapter, both Heilongjiang and Sichuan have already achieved the goal of unifying pension coordination at the provincial level. Since 2020, these two provinces have not only begun to use a single average social wage to calculate pension contribution and benefits for the entire province but also started to standardize and unify the fund account and management of its pension plans at the provincial level under the principle of the so-called two lines of income and expenditure. In consequence of these reforms, the provincial Department of Finance and the HRSS will eventually be responsible for both the collection and distribution of pension monies under the same set of regulations with a unified provincial social insurance financial account. By contrast, Guangdong has been relatively slow in raising the level of coordination, mainly due to the sharp economic disparity between the Pearl River Delta and other parts of the province. The current solution to this problem is to divide the province into four tiers of cities and to set different lower limits for cities whose average wage is lower than the provincial average. Nonetheless, this is just a temporary measure, which is scheduled to be phased out by the end of 2025.

Although the average social wage used to calculate pension benefit is quite different among the three provinces, the average per-capita benefit of the basic pension plan retirees seems to be less variable across different jurisdictions. In 2020, for example, the average monthly expenditure on each retiree was CNY 3,884, 3,006, and 3,031 for Guangdong, Heilongjiang, and Sichuan, respectively.[53] Since both the benefit calculation formula and the annual increase rate for the basic pension plans are the same in China, this result implies that some provincial governments, e.g., Heilongjiang, may have chosen to increase the benefit level through a combination of fixed-amount, indexed, or preferential adjustment. Therefore, the average replacement ratio in these provinces turns out to be higher than in other provinces in China. As described in the case study, the main reasons for Heilongjiang to provide more generous retirement benefits was to deal with its severe legacy pension debt and declining economic growth in the province. Doing so can help retirees to earn higher incomes that are more commensurate with the local living standards, but the price for this was the long-term financial health of the basic pension plans. This case also shows that, at the current stage of pension development in China, the social insurance aspect of the public pension plan is probably considered more important than other considerations. In contrast, with the relative differences in average retirement benefit across provincial governments, as revealed in the case of Sichuan, the gap between enterprise workers' and public employees' retirement benefits not only is substantial but also seems to have grown larger in the past few years. Hopefully, this upward trend will not continue in the future as long as the total number of public employees remains stable and the transition towards a unified pension system for both enterprise workers and public employees is completed on schedule.

For an array of demographic, economic, and historical reasons, the funding situation of the basic pension plans varies widely from province to province. The case study in this chapter shows that, benefiting from a prosperous economy and large inflow of young labor, the province of Guangdong currently has one of the highest funding levels and dependency ratios in China. In recent years, the province has not only been making annual surpluses at an increasing pace but also allocated a large amount of its accumulated fund balance for investment to support the national coordination program. By contrast, Heilongjiang has one of the lowest funding levels and dependency ratios in China. As a matter of fact, the province has been accumulating annual deficits since the early 2010s, and it would not be able to pay for its ongoing pension obligations if it did not receive large transfers from the central government. As explained earlier, the main contributing factors to this dire situation include a worsening economic situation, continuous loss of young people, and heavy legacy pension debt. It is worth noting that Sichuan, a province with a relatively stable economy and demographic structure, has also begun to incur annual pension deficits since 2020. Because the social pool for the basic pension plans is funded on a PAYGO basis and investment income for the plans is usually negligible, incurring an annual pension deficit means draining current workers' contributions to compensate retirees. Although the account balance accumulated from past years is large enough to cover the annual deficits, this constitutes a serious warning sign for the province and probably for the entire country as well. If a province like Sichuan has already fallen into an annual funding shortfall, many other provinces must be in the same position. One solution to that problem is the national pension coordination scheme, which has already been implemented in China since 2019, but such a solution is just temporary in nature because it will not change the declining dependency ratio and increasing pension costs that threaten the long-run fiscal health of China's pension system.

While the regulations and restrictions for investing the surplus funds in the basic pension plans are uniform for all provinces, it is up to each province to decide how to invest the pension plan surplus, whether or not to entrust the investment of its account balance to the NCSSF (since 2017), and how much of the fund balance to send to the NCSSF and for how long. Among the three provinces examined in this chapter, Guangdong participated in the pilot program as early as in 2016, and it entrusted over CNY 300 billion to the NCSSF for investing purposes in 2021. Although this already represented the largest provincial-level pension balance fund contracted out to the NCSSF, it only accounted for about 22.2% of its total accumulated account balance, even lower than the national average, which was 28% for the same year. The rest of the large fund balance of the province was invested in very conservative ways according to the "Measures on the Investment of Basic Pension Fund" issued by the State Council, earning very low returns. Some provinces, like Sichuan, had a very small fund balance for investing (CNY 13.2 billion in 2022), whereas a few other provinces, like Heilongjiang, had no fund balance to invest at all. There might be two reasons why, despite higher investment returns, most provinces are still reluctant to send more of their basic plans' fund balance to the NCSSF. First, most provincial governments lack incentives to do this because the differences in interest rates are usually unimportant for the fiscal condition of the pension plans. Second and more important, there is a fear in the provincial administrators that once the balance fund is sent to the NCSSF, it could be used by the central government for the national coordination program to cover the pension deficits of other provinces and the owner would probably never be able to recover part or all of the principal and interest.

In comparison with the two basic pension plans, the urban and rural residents' pension plans are highly similar in different places in China. As the three provinces discussed in this chapter have shown, the benefit level of this plan is usually just a small fraction of the average benefit earned by enterprise workers and public employees. Wealthier provincial or local governments may provide slightly higher base pension benefits and more generous bonuses for longer-contributing and disadvantaged plan members (e.g., old-aged, disabled, etc.), but the average benefit level is still far from enough to cover living costs after retirement. In general, most working urban and rural residents are inclined to choose the minimum contribution level that enables them to receive the base pension, but the actual contribution level may vary according to the concrete pension design of each province. For instance, most participants of this pension plan in Guangdong have chosen the lowest of the nine possible contribution levels (CNY 180/year), whereas the 4th lowest contribution level (CNY 500/year) seems to be most popular in Sichuan. Although the funding of the urban and rural residents' plan heavily relies on government subsidies, the fiscal condition of this pension plan appears to be generally good across the country. It is worth noting that, in recent years, the growth in the enrollment of this plan has slowed down. In Heilongjiang and Sichuan, the total number of participants has even been declining since 2019. One explanation for this phenomenon is that some poor urban and rural residents may no longer be able to afford the required annual contribution as the economy experiences a downturn in China. Another explanation is that as the ageing problem in China looms large, some younger residents may feel skeptical whether they will receive the promised benefit from the plan after so many years of contribution.

In sum, the three cases investigated in this chapter have illustrated many important aspects and lessons in the design, implementation, and management of the three main pension plans as the country is marching towards a unified national pension system. Based on this thorough and up-to-date case study of the three representative provinces, the next chapter moves on to discussing some of the most pressing challenges facing China's pension system.

Notes

1 State Council. 2014. Opinion on Establishing a Unified Basic Old-Age Insurance System for Urban and Rural Residents. Available at www.gov.cn/zhengce/content/2014-02/26/content_8656.htm.
2 Bureau of Statistics of Guangdong. Available at http://stats.gd.gov.cn/attachment/0/421/421380/3284464.pdf.
3 HRSS. 2021. Annual Bulletin, p. 4. Available at http://hrss.gd.gov.cn/attachment/0/494/494044/3975371.pdf.
4 Guangdong Bureau of Statistics. Available at http://stats.gd.gov.cn/attachment/0/421/421314/3283438.pdf.
5 China Enterprise Social Insurance White Paper. Available at www.51shebao.com/news/industry_report/1.
6 Shen, Yan. September 5, 2018. Analysis: China's Social Security from the Strict Levy Triggered by the Burden of Enterprises to Increase the Worry of

Tax Cuts Can Be Clearly Understood? Available at www.reuters.com/article/
social-security-corporate-analysis-0905-idCNKCS1LL0RV.

7   See "Implementation Plan for Improving the Provincial Coordination of Basic
    Pension Insurance for Enterprise Employees in Guangdong Province", 2017.
    Available at www.gd.gov.cn/gkmlpt/content/0/146/post_146147. html#7; "Opin-
    ions of Guangdong Province on the Implementation of the Provincial Coordina-
    tion System for Standardizing Basic Pension Insurance for Enterprise Employees",
    2020. Available at http://hrss.gd.gov.cn/gkmlpt/content/3/3230/post_3230104.
    html#4033.

8   Every year, the province issued a notice to announce the average wages for the four
    city groups, but there was no change in some years for the purpose of calculating
    lower bounds.

9   This was based on the average wage of previous years. It did not change until Janu-
    ary 1, 2018.

10 "Opinions about Standardizing the Implementation of the Provincial Coordination
    of the Guangdong's Enterprise Workers' Basic Pension Plan". Available at http://
    hrss.gd.gov.cn/gkmlpt/content/3/3230/post_3230104.html#4033.

11 "Notice on Adjustment of Retiree's Basic Pension in 2022". Available at www.gov.
    cn/zhengce/zhengceku/2022-05/26/content_5692437.htm.

12 "The HRSS of Guangdong's Letter in Response to the Recommendation of No.
    1632 Delegate of the Third Session of the Thirteenth National People's Con-
    gress". Available at http://hrss.gd.gov.cn/gkmlpt/content/3/3025/post_3025847.
    html#1291.

13 Ibid.

14 "Notice of the People's Government of Guangdong Province on the Implementa-
    tion of the Decision of the State Council on the Reform of the Pension Insurance
    System for Staff of Institutions and Agencies". Available at www.gd.gov.cn/zwgk/
    wjk/zcfgk/content/post_2713146.html.

15 The HRSS of Guangdong Province, multiple years, "Statistical Bulletin on the
    Development of Social Security". Available at http://hrss.gd.gov.cn/zwgk/sjfb/
    index.html.

16 "Implementation Measures of Basic Pension Insurance for Urban and Rural Resi-
    dents in Guangdong Province". Available at www.gd.gov.cn/zwgk/jhgh/content/
    post_2793692.html.

17 "Minimum Standard of Basic Pension for Urban and Rural Residents in Guangdong
    Province Increased". Available at http://hrss.gd.gov.cn/gkmlpt/content/3/3997/
    post_3997784.html#1274.

18 "Social Insurance Information Disclosure in Guangdong Province in 2016". Avail-
    able at http://hrss.gd.gov.cn/zwgk/sjfb/content/post_2729190.html.

19 Assuming minimum government subsidy and zero interest on the account balance.

20 This increased from CNY 180 in 2021 to CNY 190 per month on July 1, 2022.
    See "Minimum Standard of Basic Pension for Urban and Rural Residents in
    Guangdong Province Increased". Available at http://hrss.gd.gov.cn/gkmlpt/
    content/3/3997/post_3997784.html#1274.

21 "Yunfu Municipal People's Government's Notice on the Implementation of the
    'Guangdong Province Urban and Rural Residents Basic Pension Insurance Imple-
    mentation Measures'". Available at www.yunfu.gov.cn/rsj/zwgk/zcfgyjd/content/
    post_1354519.html.

22 National Bureau of Statistics of China. Available at www.stats.gov.cn/english/.

23 China Daily. February 17, 2017. Available at www.chinadaily.com.cn/interface/
    baidu/1120781/2017-2-17/cd_28161841.html.

24 Available at http://hrss.hlj.gov.cn/hrss/gkzd/public_zfxxgk.shtml?tab=gkzd.

25 Available at http://tjj.hlj.gov.cn/tjj/c106749/common_zfxxgk.shtml?tab=zdgknr.

26 The Beijing News. 13 Regions Have Less Than One Year of Pension Payment Capacity Heilongjiang Has a Shortfall of More Than 20 Billion Dollars. Available at https://finance.sina.cn/china/gncj/2017-12-10/detail-ifyppemf6155976.d.html.

27 "Heilongjiang Statistical Yearbook 2018". Available at http://tjj.hlj.gov.cn/tjj/c106782/201902/c00_30326285.shtml.

28 "Interim Measures for Provincial Collections and Expenditures of the Basic Pension Insurance Fund for Enterprise Employees". Available at www.hlj.gov.cn/hlj/c107956/202002/c00_30645448.shtml.

29 "The HRSS of Heilongjiang Province and Heilongjiang Provincial Department of Finance on the 2020 Adjustment of Basic Pension for Retirees Participating in Basic Pension Insurance for Enterprise Employees". Available at www.waizi. org. cn/policy/88912.html.

30 "The Thirteenth Five-Year Plan for the Development of Human Resources and Social Security in Heilongjiang Province". Available at http://hrss.hlj.gov.cn/hrss/c111785/201612/30646872/files/1608767353491003257.pdf.

31 Huanqiu Net. January 14, 2019. Southern Pension Balance to Support the Northeast? Heilongjiang Pension of 2,119 Yuan. Available at https://china.huanqiu.com/article/9CaKrnKhmnc.

32 "State Council's Approval on Agreeing to the Pilot Implementation Program of Improving Urban Social Security System in Heilongjiang Province". Available at www.gov.cn/gongbao/content/2004/content_62829.htm.

33 Ibid.

34 "Annual Report of the National Social Security Fund Council Fund for 2015". Available at www.ssf.gov.cn/portal/jjcw/sbjjndbg/webinfo/2016/06/1632636003321600.htm.

35 "Heilongjiang Province Focuses on 'Four' and Continuously Improves the Level of Urban and Rural Residents' Pension Insurance Services and Protection". Available at www.hlj.gov.cn/hlj/c107857/202303/c00_31554494.shtml.

36 It went up from CNY 660 (55/month) in 2014 and CNY 960 (80/month) in 2017.

37 "Heilongjiang Province Opinions on the Implementation of the Mechanism for Determining Basic Pension Insurance Benefits and Normal Adjustment of Basic Pension for Urban and Rural Residents". Available at https://m12333.cn/policy/mbyk.html.

38 "Heilongjiang Province Focuses on 'Four' and Continuously Improves the Level of Urban and Rural Residents' Pension Insurance Services and Protection". Available at www.hlj.gov.cn/hlj/c107857/202303/c00_31554494.shtml.

39 "Annual Report of the National Social Security Fund Council Fund for 2015". Available at www.ssf.gov.cn/portal/jjcw/sbjjndbg/webinfo/2016/06/1632636003321600.htm.

40 National Bureau of Statistics of China. Available at https://data.stats.gov.cn/easyquery.htm?cn=E0103.

41 Sohu. March 16, 2020. Sichuan's Population Movement Characteristics Revealed, Which Cities Are Experiencing Serious Population Outflows? Available at www.sohu.com/a/380437884_120179484.

42 China News. June 23, 2022. Henan, Anhui, and Sichuan Are Home to More Than 10 Million People, Mainly Going to These Places. Available at www.chinanews.com.cn/cj/2022/06-23/9786548.shtml.

43 The People's Government of Sichuan. 2021. 83.675 Million People! Sichuan's Resident Population Is the Fifth Largest in China! The Latest Population Figures for 21 Cities and States Are Out!". Available at www.sc.gov.cn/10462/10464/10797/2021/5/26/4639ee4365934ece91fd3b33f70bfda0.shtml.

44 "Sichuan Provincial People's Government: Notice on Regulating the Provincial Coordination System of Basic Pension Insurance for Enterprise Employees". Available at www.sc.gov.cn/10462/zfwjts/2020/11/24/777f3d8744404d7a-97ce182656623102.shtml.

45 "Notice on the issuance of the 'Fourteenth Five-Year Plan' for the Development of Human Resources and Social Security in Sichuan Province". Available at http://rst.sc.gov.cn/rst/zcwj/2021/9/2/70e153ff844d400f8d35869198b7e09a.shtml.

46 "Sichuan Provincial People's Government: Notice on Regulating the Provincial Coordination System of Basic Pension Insurance for Enterprise Employees". Available at www.sc.gov.cn/10462/zfwjts/2020/11/24/777f3d8744404d7a-97ce18 2656623102.shtml.

47 Ibid.

48 "Implementing Opinions on Establishing a Unified Basic Pension Insurance System for Urban and Rural Residents". Available at http://rst.sc.gov.cn/rst/ylbxjwjzc wj/2022/8/12/65301b0102e147b29a7d005f1a67283f.shtml.

49 Ibid.

50 Available at http://rst.sc.gov.cn/rst/zcwj/2021/9/2/70e153ff844d400f8d35869198b 7e09a.shtml.

51 Available at www.sc.gov.cn/10462/10464/13722/2022/11/4/9d3169b545fd482ebe cba57b40f3806b.shtml.

52 "Statistical Bulletin on the Development of Human Resources and Social Security in Sichuan Province in 2021". Available at http://rst.sc.gov.cn/rst/ghtj/2022/7/19/3 ac847eeb00f438b8dd65bdb40b1ca23.shtml.

53 The total pension expenditure figure includes some small administrative costs, so the actual benefit that each retiree receives is slightly lower than these numbers.

4   Challenges facing the Chinese pension system

As with any pension plans that are funded on a PAYGO basis, the most important long-term concern is the sustainability of the pension plan, i.e., whether the expected revenues can pay for the expected pension benefits in the distant future. Just like most countries in the industrialized world, Chinese public pension plans are facing a long-term sustainability problem, except that the problem is more acute in China than in most other countries. At the heart of the sustainability issue in a PAYGO pension plan is a country's demographics, i.e., the ratio of contributing workers to benefit recipients, which is decidedly working against the Chinese public pension's sustainability over the next few decades. Another more unique factor working against Chinese sustainability is the large historical legacy pension debt that is hidden and that is growing in size due to the cumulative interest on the debt. The sustainability issue is also exacerbated by lax efforts in collecting pension contributions in the past. In addition to the sustainability issue, there is a second challenge facing Chinese public pension plans due to the fragmentation of pension plans for urban workers. The third major challenge is the imbalance of the overall pension system, with a heavy reliance on the first pillar, relatively little contribution from the second pillar, and almost no contribution from the third pillar, of an ideal pension system. In this chapter, we address these three broad categories of challenges facing the Chinese pension system.

4.1   Challenge 1: Sustainability

Of the three challenges, the biggest challenge by far is the sustainability issue, primarily as a result of population ageing but also due to inadequate revenue collection and legacy pension debt.

4.1.1   Demographics

Demographics is decidedly working against Chinese public pension plans. The Chinese population is ageing at an increasing pace. This quickening pace is

DOI: 10.4324/9781003091974-4

primarily due to two long-term demographic trends: the increasing life expectancy and the decreasing fertility rate, chiefly as a result of the one-child policy implemented in the late seventies. Unless otherwise noted, all population-related data in this chapter are from the United Nations World Population Projects 2022.[1]

4.1.1.1 Life expectancy

Since the founding of the People's Republic of China in 1949, life expectancy has been steadily increasing. It was less than 44 prior to 1950, a reflection of not just poverty but also decades of civil wars and anti-Japanese combat during World War II. With no war in China since 1949 and the availability of basic health care, gains in life expectancy were easy to obtain. The more impressive gains in life expectancy occurred after the end of the Cultural Revolution in 1976, when China implemented opening and reform policies that led to decades of fast economic growth, turning China into an upper middle-income country and the second largest economy in the world. Between 1975 and 2020, the life expectancy increased by 17 years to 78 years old, on par with that of most industrialized countries. According to United Nations projections, it is likely to continue to increase over the next several decades. By 2050, it will increase to 83.75. In other words, over a 100-year period, China's life expectancy will almost double from 44 to 84. With that kind of life expectancy, there will be a lot of elderly people. Figure 4.1 gives China's life expectancy between 1950 and 2050.[2]

One very direct impact of this persistent increase in life expectancy on public pensions is the payments from individual accounts. As explained in

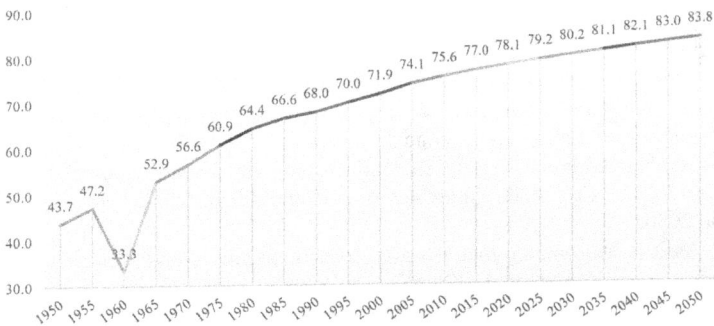

Figure 4.1 Life Expectancy in China

Source: United Nations World Population Projects 2022.

Chapter 2, when a man retires at the age of 60, the balance in his individual account will be paid out to him over 139 months (or until he reaches about 71 years old). After that, the account will be exhausted, but he will continue to be paid the same amount from the social pool. For a woman, that individual account will be exhausted at the age of 66 if she retires at the age of 50. Even using the average life expectancy of 78 in 2020, that means the man will continue to be paid this amount for another seven years, and the woman will be paid for another 12 years. As the life expectancy continues to increase, they will most likely be paid for more years beyond that. While 139 months for men and 195 months for women might have been appropriate when the system was first designed at the beginning of this century, life expectancy has since increased, but there has been no corresponding increase in the number of months to draw down the account balance. It should be recognized that the funding for such continuous payments beyond the exhaustion date has never been set aside, meaning that it will all come from current employer contributions into the social pooling part of the pension plan. This alone will drain resources from the social pooling, thus worsening its financial health.

4.1.1.2 *Fertility rate*

The fertility rate, however, exhibits a very different growth trend. Fertility refers to the number of births per woman in a population. In 1950, China had an extraordinarily high fertility rate of 6, and it held steady around 6 for 20 years until 1970. This was most likely due to the rural nature of Chinese society (the vast majority of the people lived in rural areas, where high birth rates were a norm) and also the exhortation by the Chinese government to women to have more children. Since the middle of Cultural Revolution, the fertility rate has followed a long-term downward trend. Initially, this probably reflected the disruption the Cultural Revolution caused in the lives of young people. Soon after the end of Cultural Revolution, the Chinese government started implementing its one-child policy around 1980, although with exemptions, especially for couples living in rural areas. By the early 1990s, the fertility rate had stabilized around 1.6. Even though the one-child policy has been relaxed several times in the second decade of the 21st century, the fertility rate has not budged much, and it will continue on a downward trend, stabilizing around 1.3–1.4 till 2050. Figure 4.2 gives China's fertility rate between 1950 and 2050.

As it is well-known that a fertility rate of slightly above 2 is needed to keep the population stable, China's persistent fertility rate of well below 2 between 1990 and 2050 means the population will eventually shrink. As widely reported, the Chinese National Bureau of Statistics announced in January 2023 that China's population declined by 850,000 in 2022 to 1.41 billion, the first drop in population since the early 1960s. According to the United

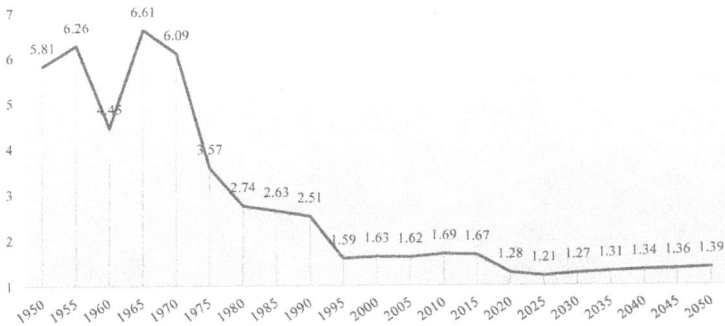

Figure 4.2 Historical Trend of Chinese Fertility Rate

Source: United Nations World Population Projects 2022.

Nations forecast, China's population will gradually decline, and by 2050, it will go down to 1.313 billion. This United Nations projection about Chinese population decline was also confirmed by another projection from a demographic forecasting team at the Shanghai Academy of Social Sciences. It projected that the Chinese population would start declining in 2022 at an annual rate of 1.1% and that by 2100, its population will be down to 587 million, less than half of that in 2021 (Peng, 2022).

4.1.1.3   *Population ageing*

These two demographic trends of China create a perfect storm for the ageing of population, with more and more elderly people due to longer life expectancy and fewer and fewer younger people due to lower fertility, and eventually, a shrinking population. The best measurement of the ageing of population is elderly people, typically 65 years old and above, as a percentage of the population. However, since men can retire at the age of 60, and women at an even younger age, we also need to look at people 60 years old and above as a percentage of the population. Figure 4.3 gives these two percentages in China between 1950 and 2050.

These two trend lines tell a very similar story, and thus, we just use the 65-years-old-and-above age group as an example. As can be seen, this percentage did not change much until the 21st century. Between 1950 and 2000, it went from 5.0% to 6.9%. Over the next 20 years, it still went up by a relatively small 6 percentage points to 12.6% in 2020. After 2020, however, this percentage should start to increase at a much faster pace, and by 2050, 30% of the population will be over 65.

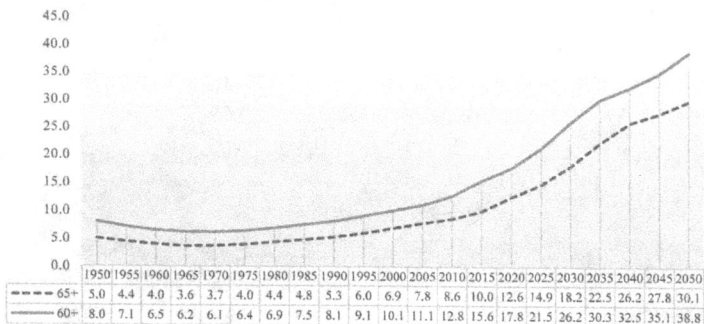

	1950	1955	1960	1965	1970	1975	1980	1985	1990	1995	2000	2005	2010	2015	2020	2025	2030	2035	2040	2045	2050
65+	5.0	4.4	4.0	3.6	3.7	4.0	4.4	4.8	5.3	6.0	6.9	7.8	8.6	10.0	12.6	14.9	18.2	22.5	26.2	27.8	30.1
60+	8.0	7.1	6.5	6.2	6.1	6.4	6.9	7.5	8.1	9.1	10.1	11.1	12.8	15.6	17.8	21.5	26.2	30.3	32.5	35.1	38.8

Figure 4.3 Historical Trend of Elderly People as a Percentage of Population (%)

Source: United Nations World Population Projects 2022.

Even though other parts of world exhibit similar ageing processes, China will age at a faster pace in the future. As comparison, while the U.S. population is also ageing, it will age at a slower pace in the future. In 2020, the share of the old age population (65 years and older) was 16.2% in the United States, higher than China's 12.6%. The U.S. percentage will continue to be higher than that of China until they reach parity at around 21.5% in 2034. By 2050, even though the U.S. percentage will only grow to 23.6%, China's percentage will be 30%. In other words, China's percentage will increase by almost 140% between 2020 and 2050, whereas that of the United States will increase by only 45% over the same period.

Having more elderly people in retirement certainly puts a lot of strain on the pension system. Since public pensions, like the basic pension plans in China, are funded on a PAYGO basis, what also matters is the ratio of working-age people to retirees, or for every pension beneficiary, how many potential workers are contributing. The higher the number, the better the funding situation. Sometimes this is also expressed as the ratio of retirees over working-age people. While it is customary to use 65 as the cutoff age for retirees vs. workers, we also use 60 as another cutoff age, for the reason mentioned earlier. We compare the elderly in the 60+ age group with people in the 20–59 age range, and we compare the 65+ group with people in the 20–64 age group. Figure 4.4 displays these two ratios.

These two ratios show similar trends. They both remained fairly stable between 1950 and 2000 and then took off after that, similar to the trend of population ageing shown in Figure 4.3. The difference is that the slope is steeper here, reflecting not only population ageing but also a shrinking workforce. For the 65+ age group, as recently as 2000, there were as many as ten workers supporting one elderly person. By 2020, about five workers

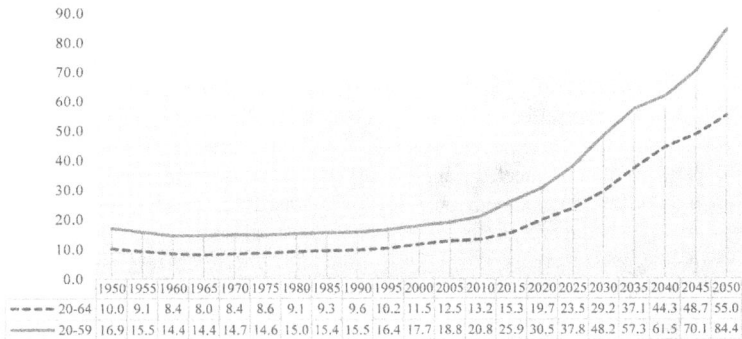

	1950	1955	1960	1965	1970	1975	1980	1985	1990	1995	2000	2005	2010	2015	2020	2025	2030	2035	2040	2045	2050
20-64	10.0	9.1	8.4	8.0	8.4	8.6	9.1	9.3	9.6	10.2	11.5	12.5	13.2	15.3	19.7	23.5	29.2	37.1	44.3	48.7	55.0
20-59	16.9	15.5	14.4	14.4	14.7	14.6	15.0	15.4	15.5	16.4	17.7	18.8	20.8	25.9	30.5	37.8	48.2	57.3	61.5	70.1	84.4

Figure 4.4 Ratio of Elderly (60+/65+) to Working-Age Population (20–59/64) (%)

Source: United Nations World Population Projects 2022.

supported one elderly person. However, by 2050, only about two workers will support one elderly person. Thus, over a 100-year period, there will be an 80% drop in this support ratio.

While using the 65+ age group of as a proxy for retirees works in many other countries, it is not the case in China, as most people can retire before the age of 60. To make matters worse, early retirement is fairly common in China for many reasons. The MOHRSS reported in 2012 that the average retirement age in China was around 53.[3] While the average retirement age may have increased since 2012, it probably will not be by much since the legal retirement age has not been increased. To get a more realistic picture of the ratio of retirees to the working age population, we need to lower the age for retirees (or elderly people). Since the actual average retirement age is not available, we use 60 as the cutoff age for these two groups, even though this is much higher than the average retirement age reported for 2012. As expected, this is a much higher ratio. This ratio was just around 30% in 2020, and it will rise all the way to about 85% in 2050. This means that in 2020, about 3.4 potential workers supported one retiree, and by 2050, only 1.2 potential workers will support one retire. Had the actual average retirement age been lower than 60, this ratio most likely would be very close to parity by 2050. This is obviously a trend for the entire country. Since China has three different pension plans and the biggest of the three, in terms of cost, is the pension plan for urban enterprise workers, we are also more concerned about the ratio for this plan. As Chapter 2 shows, this ratio is even worse for this plan. For 2021, the latest year such data were available, the ratio was about 2.65, lower than the 3.4 for the whole country in 2020. If we use the national trend projection as a guide, then it is certainly possible that only one worker will support one retiree in this plan by 2050 in the best-case scenario.

4.1.2   *Reduction in pension plan revenue*

The sustainability challenge as a result of demographic changes is made worse by the widening gap between the revenue that is needed to meet this challenge and the actual revenue collected. Normally, when a pension plan's cost is going up, the expected response would be to increase revenue within the pension plan to meet the increasing cost. However, this is not the case in China with the basic pension plan, for at least three reasons. This discussion about pension revenue is exclusively concerned with the pension plan for urban enterprise workers, the biggest of the three public pension plans.

First, the central government, fully aware of the long-term sustainability challenge of this pension plan, actually reduced the employer contribution rate. As mentioned earlier, the employer contribution to the social pool of pension plan used to be 20% prior to 2019. Admittedly, this was one of the highest contribution rates paid by employers in the world and thus represented a considerable burden on employers, affecting their international competitiveness as well as providing an incentive for them to avoid paying the full amount. As a result, to stimulate the economy, the Chinese government permanently reduced the employer contribution rate to 16% in 2019, equivalent to a drop of 20% in annual contribution revenue, reflected in a significant drop in the plan's revenue between 2019 and 2020.

This contrarian policy move on the part of Chinese central government in one way reflects one unique nature of this public pension plan in China. As discussed in the introduction in the first chapter, a public pension plan should have its own dedicated funding source requiring no subsidy from government's general taxes. In other words, it should be self-sustaining. By reducing rather than increasing the employer contribution rate when more revenue was needed, the Chinese government did not treat this pension plan as self-sustaining. While providing financial security during retirement is an important purpose of this plan, the Chinese government also treated it as part of its toolkit to develop the Chinese economy. This partly reflects the mixed economic model of China, where economic planning is still practiced by the central government. In this respect, the Chinese government does not treat the finance of this pension plan as totally separate from the rest of government finance, knowing full well that a reduction in employer contributions will lead to a bigger funding gap down the road. This means that the government will need to find other resources to plug the funding gap, possibly more tax subsidy, with or without benefit reduction.

While the first reason for the widening revenue gap has to do with government policy, the second reason has to do with employers themselves. In China, many employers do not make pension contributions based on the actual salary base. Because of the nominally high employer contribution rate and the discretion employers have in determining the salary base on which the contribution is made, between 60% and 300% of the average local wages, employers contribute an amount that is typically less than an amount based on the actual salary base. Since in many places, it is the agency responsible for Social Security programs that collects the contributions, rather than the tax administration agency, it is not easy for the agency to verify the real salary base. According to one estimate, the salary base on which the contribution was made was 81.5% of the real salary base in 2000, down to 72.2% in 2006, and 63% in 2015 (Zhao and Mi, 2019). Another dataset shows how widespread this problem is. May 1st Social Security, a business consultancy group, has been publishing a "White Paper on Chinese Enterprises' Social Security" since 2013. One data point it provides is the percentage of enterprises that fully comply with the salary base for employer contributions. From 2017 to 2021, these percentages were 24%, 27%, 30%, 31%, and 30%, respectively. It should be noted that the employer contribution rate was reduced from 20% to 16% in the middle of 2019, and this was fully implemented in 2020. Despite this reduction, there was no meaningful increase in the percentage of enterprises that fully complied with the regulation on salary base in 2021. Noncompliance on such a scale inevitably leads to significant revenue loss for the basic pension plans.

The third reason for the widening gap has to do with employees themselves. Many participants stop contributing after 15 years as a result of the longstanding policy. As explained earlier, an employee can qualify for basic public pension after 15 years of contribution. There are participants who stop contributing to the system after 15 years of contribution, and their employers are certainly happy to comply with such a wish, as it also eliminates their obligation to contribute. For comparison, the Social Security program in the United States requires workers to contribute as long as they earn wages and salaries. Thus, the number of actual contributors is less than the number of active participants in basic pension plans, and the ratio of active contributors to active participants has been declining for quite some time. Around 2010, 10% of active participants were non-contributors, and by 2020, 20% of active participants were non-contributors, leading to a loss of revenue to the tune of CNY 2.6 trillion over this ten-year period (Li, 2021).

In summary, all three parties involved in pension plan financing have contributed to the widening gap between what needs to be collected to finance this pension plan and what is actually collected, given the current pension benefits.

4.1.3 *Long-term funding gap*

What does this all mean for the long-term sustainability of the pension plan for urban workers? Unlike the U.S. Social Security program, whose trustees have to perform a 75-year actuarial valuation of the program every year to understand its funding situation into the distant future, neither the Chinese central government nor the provincial governments perform actuarial valuations of the pension plan(s) for urban workers. This job is left to governmental and nongovernmental research institutions. One of the most reputable governmental institutions is the Chinese Academy of Social Sciences, which has been performing actuarial valuations on China's basic pension plan for urban workers for many years, and the latest one was performed for the period between 2019 and 2050 (Chinese Academy of Social Sciences, 2019). According to this actuarial valuation, total annual revenue (including contribution, government revenue transfer, and investment income) will continue to exceed total annual expenditure till 2027. (It should be noted that if not for the government revenue transfer, the plan's own revenue source of contribution and investment income became less than total expenditure in 2014; see Table 2.6 in Chapter 2.) As a matter of fact, according to Zheng (2022), total revenue transfer from all levels of government between 1998 and 2021 amounted to CNY 6.5 trillion, whereas the cumulative balance of basic pension plans was CNY 5.26 trillion in 2021. In other words, if not for the revenue transfer, the basic pension plan would have a cumulative deficit of CNY 1.14 trillion. This is another strong indicator of the uniqueness of Chinese public pension plan financing. It was never meant to be a fully standalone pension plan that could sustain on its system's own revenue source. From a national perspective, there has never been a clear separation between pension financing and other government revenue sources, chiefly general tax revenues.

Due to the annual surplus, the cumulative balance will continue to grow and peak at about CNY 7 trillion in 2027. In 2028, the system will run its first annual deficit of CNY 118 billion, and this annual deficit will grow to CNY 11.28 trillion by 2050. Without the current government subsidy, the deficit will be CNY 16.75 trillion in 2050 (implying a revenue transfer of about CNY 5.5 trillion in 2050 already baked into the government budgets at all levels). Initially, the annual deficit can be covered by the cumulative balance. By 2035, this cumulative balance will be exhausted. The cumulative deficit between 2035 and 2050 will be CNY 86.8 trillion.

4.1.4   Legacy debt and the related "empty individual account" problem

The sustainability of the basic pension plans has also been exacerbated by the legacy pension debt and the resultant empty individual accounts problem. The legacy debt resulted from the transition from the old pension system to a new pension system, as discussed in Chapter 2. When the new system was launched, there was never any indication how this legacy debt should be funded, implying that this legacy debt would be paid by intergenerational transfers of funds, meaning that current workers will pay for current retirees' benefits and so on so forth. Of course, any transition to or setup of a new pension system funded on a PAYGO basis will incur legacy debt, as in the case of the Social Security program established in the United States in 1935. The problem with China's legacy debt is that it is much bigger, for at least two reasons. First, it happened much later after the establishment of the old pension system, and since the Chinese population grew at a much faster pace during the old pension system's existence than it is growing now, that means there are a lot of workers retiring from the old system and now receiving benefits under the new pension system. Second, since the transition happened so much later, the life expectancy is now also much higher than before. Life expectancy was already around 70 in 1997, but it increased further to 78 in 2020, whereas the retirement ages for men and women are still at 60 and 50 (55) respectively. That means not just that more people are receiving benefits without contribution but also that these people are receiving these benefits for a much longer period of time. As comparison, the life expectancy in the United States in 1935, when the Social Security program was first established, was 60 for men and 64 for women, and both men and women had to be 65 before they were eligible for normal Social Security benefits.[4] Therefore, the Social Security program's legacy debt should be much smaller than that for China's basic pension plan for urban workers. Even though there has never been an official estimate of the size of this legacy debt, there were quite a few academic ones. One estimate (Liu, 2008) put the transition cost (or the legacy debt) at CNY 8 trillion.

The cumulative balance of the urban workers' basic pension plan, in theory, should include the balance of both social pooling and individual accounts. In reality, due to the mostly empty individual accounts, the cumulative balance of basic plans reflects the balance in social pooling in most places. The question then becomes what the balance of individual accounts should be if they were fully funded and invested to earn income. According to one estimate, at the end of 2011, the empty accounts totaled CNY 2.2 trillion, equal to nearly 90% of the total funds recorded in individual accounts, and equivalent to 114% of the total balance of the basic pension fund (Zuo, 2013). The Chinese Academy of Social Sciences' 2019 actuarial valuation put this balance of all individual accounts at CNY 7.65 trillion, equal to 8% of China's GDP. It is not known how much of that amount was actually funded in individual accounts.

To make matters worse, these individual accounts are supposed to be fully funded and invested. With empty accounts, there are no funds to be invested to earn income in the future. Because these accounts are still credited with interest every year, they really exist in name only, and thus, they are notional individual accounts. As described in Chapter 2, for most years since they were established, the interest rate credit was mostly tied to short-term bank deposit rates, which were fairly low most years. Since 2016, the central government has dictated one book-keeping interest rate to all basic plans' individual accounts across the country. The average rate was 7.5% between 2016 and

2020, which was much higher than the bank deposit rate. While this high rate will ensure that individual accounts will grow a lot faster in value, it also creates enormous pressure on the governments at all levels, as these notional account balances will eventually have to be paid by the pension plan itself or more likely by government revenue transfers at all levels.

4.1.5   Declining replacement ratio

The replacement ratio of basic pension plans has been on a long-term decline. As discussed in Chapter 2, the replacement ratio based on the combination of social pooling and individual account was initially expected to be 59% in 2005. This was a policy goal at that time rather than a legal stipulation. There are two ways of measuring the replacement ratio in China's context. The first measurement is to compare a person' pension benefit at the time of retirement to his/her salary prior to retirement. The MOHRSS's goal of 59% most likely referred to this measurement. As discussed in Chapter 2, this pension benefit is partially based on the local average salary. This makes the growth rate in local average salary an important factor in determining whether this replacement ratio can stay constant in retirement. Since a retiree in China on average will receive pension benefits for another two decades after retirement, a second and potentially more important measurement is to compare the pension benefit against local average wage during years in retirement, not just at the time of retirement, i.e., the long-term trend of replacement ratio. While such data are not available for individual retirees at the local level, they are available in aggregate at the national level. This can be measured by comparing the national average pension benefit to the national average labor income in a particular year. One measure of national average benefit is simply the ratio of the total annual pension expenditure to the number of retirees, and such data are available in Tables 2–5 and 2–6. China's State Statistics Bureau publishes annual data on average salary for employed personnel in urban areas. Figure 4.5 presents the trend of this ratio of average pension benefit to average salary during a 20-year period between 2001 and 2021.

As can be seen from this trend, the replacement ratio has been on a long-term decline, from about 65% in 2002 to 40% in 2021, although the pace of decline has been uneven. It experienced a significant drop in the first few years of this period, then stabilized in the middle of this period, and then experienced another significant drop beginning in 2016. This trend largely reflects the difference between the growth rates of average pension benefit and average salary. It dropped significantly in the beginning because the pension benefit grew a lot more slowly than average salary. That is why the central government established the policy of setting an annual growth rate in pension benefit beginning in 2006, as Table 2.1 shows. Between 2006 and 2015, the annual growth rate was set at 10%, except for the 24% rate in 2006, presumably to make up for the low growth rates in pension benefit in the

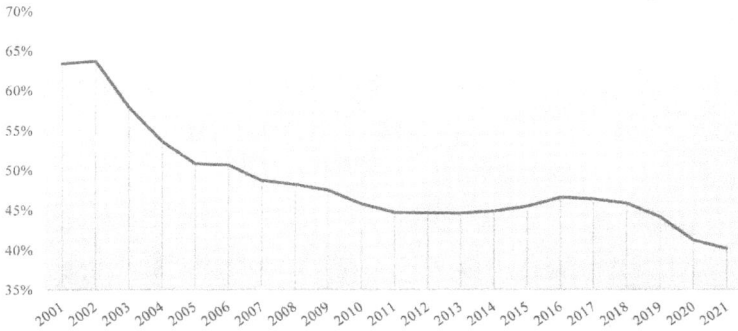

Figure 4.5 Historical Trend of Replacement Ratio
Source: MOHRSS and the State Statistics Bureau.

many years prior to 2006. As 10% was close to the average salary growth rate of about 13% in these years, it stabilized the replacement ratio at around 45% in these years. Since 2016, the central government has substantially reduced the growth rate in pension benefit. The average growth rate between 2016 and 2021 was 5%, as Table 2.1 shows, even though the average salary growth rate during this period was still around 10%, leading to the significant drop in the replacement ratio during this period.

It is not difficult to understand why this replacement ratio has been declining. The main reason is the increasing funding pressure on basic pension plans due to population ageing and policy changes, such as the central government's decision to reduce the employer contribution rate from 20% to 16%. As a result of this funding pressure, the growth rate in annual pension benefit, set by the central government annually, has declined significantly in recent years. Consequently, it can no longer keep up with wage growth in the broader economy, leading to the decline in replacement ratio of public pension benefit over time. As the funding for any increase in pension benefit post retirement will have to come out of the basic plan itself, one way to relieve the financial pressure on pension plans is to reduce the growth rate in pension benefit to a level below the wage growth rate in the economy. This finding on declining replacement ratio is buttressed by other studies. For example, Wang (2019) found that the replacement ratio was less than 50% in the second decade of this century. As the basic pension plan faces a chronic funding shortage nationwide going forward, the pension benefit's replacement ratio is more likely to decline even further in the future, unless the wage growth slows down dramatically in the overall Chinese economy.

Table 4.1 shows the average replacement ratio for men and women in OECD countries as well as their pension contribution rates.

Table 4.1 Replacement Ratio and Contribution Rate in OECD Countries

Country	Replacement Ratio for a Male at Average Wage	Replacement Ratio for a Female at Average Wage	Contribution Rate for an Average Worker
Australia	31.3	28.4	9.5
Austria	74.1	74.1	22.8
Belgium	43.4	43.4	16.4
Canada	38.8	38.8	10.5
Chile	31.2	28.8	12.8
Colombia	74.8	73.4	14.1
Costa Rica	71.9	71.9	13.5
Czech Republic	49.0	49.0	28.0
Denmark	80.0	80.0	12.8
Estonia	28.0	28.0	20.0
Finland	56.6	56.6	22.4
France	60.2	60.2	27.8
Germany	41.5	41.5	18.6
Greece	72.6	72.6	26.5
Hungary	62.5	58.1	21.8
Iceland	51.8	51.8	21.9
Ireland	29.7	29.7	15.1
Israel	41.5	34.1	19.2
Italy	74.6	74.6	33.0
Japan	32.4	32.4	18.3
Korea	31.2	31.2	9.0
Latvia	43.4	43.4	20.0
Lithuania	19.7	19.7	8.7
Luxembourg	76.6	76.6	16.0
Mexico	61.2	58.2	6.3
Netherlands	69.7	69.7	25.1
Norway	46.0	46.0	23.2
Poland	30.6	23.4	19.5
Portugal	74.9	74.9	22.7
Slovak Republic	53.1	53.1	22.8
Slovenia	42.0	42.0	24.4
Spain	73.9	73.9	28.3
Sweden	53.3	53.3	22.3
Switzerland	44.1	43.5	17.0
Turkey	73.3	70.3	20.0
United Kingdom	49.0	49.0	20.4
United States	39.2	39.2	10.6
OECD—Average	51.8	50.9	18.2

Source: OECD, Pensions at a Glance 2021.

Compared to China, the average replacement ratio in OECD countries is higher, and at the same time, the average contribution rate is lower. For countries with similar contribution rate to China's, the replacement ratio tends to be higher. Compared to OECD countries, China is thus in the unenviable position of having a low replacement ratio but a high contribution rate. Such a situation has at least two explanations. First, the relatively high contribution rate was needed to generate revenue to pay off the very large legacy debt, and second, pervasive noncompliance with the real salary base for employer contributions, partly as a result of the high employer contribution rate, resulted in less revenue for the pension plans and, thus, a lower replacement ratio over time.

4.2 Challenge 2: Fragmentation of urban worker pension plans

Prior to 2021, there were literally thousands of pension plans for urban workers across China at the local level. Even after 2021, there are still 31 provincial pension plans for urban workers. A unified national plan, despite some central government effort, still remains a goal at this point. In this section, we discuss the root cause of this fragmentation and the challenges it creates, chiefly the inequity in financing among provinces, the inefficiency in governance, and the treatment of migrant workers.

4.2.1 Causes of fragmentation

The root cause of fragmentation in the pension plans across the country has to do with the pension benefit design from the very beginning. When the central government first established the new pension plan for urban workers, it decided that such a plan would be administered locally, i.e., primarily at the county or city level, rather than at the provincial or national level. This was done for multiple reasons. First, as explained in the first chapter, China typically starts major reform with pilot programs at the local level to minimize the "sunk cost" of any major policy failure. The late Chinese paramount leader Deng Xiaoping summarized this approach perfectly, calling it "crossing the river by touching the stones". Therefore, for something like a public pension, it makes perfect sense to start at the county/municipal level. Besides, at the beginning of this experiment in the early eighties, the central government did not have the relevant expertise, such as actuarial science, and administrative capacity to manage a nationwide public pension system. It thus gave local governments some latitude in designing their own public pension plans, such as pension benefit levels and contribution rates.

Second, administration at the local level also aligns incentives better with responsibilities. Responsibilities refer to local governments' obligation to pay pension benefits to retired workers, whereas incentives refer to local governments' desire to collect revenue to pay for the pension benefits. Due to the transition from an enterprise-based pension system to a public pension plan, such transition costs can vary significantly from one local government to another and from one province to another, as many of these enterprises used to be run by the local governments prior to the eighties. Therefore, the local governments would have been more eager to collect the necessary revenue to pay for their own obligations. It would not be hard to imagine that had some of the funds collected at the local level been transferred to other parts of the country to pay for their pension benefits, then the local governments would not have had the strongest incentive to collect the amount required. In other words, it could have led to a moral hazard problem.[5]

Third, and somewhat related to this previous reason, China is a big country, in terms of both size and population. That inevitably leads to economic disparity not only among different provinces but also within provinces. There is economic disparity in every country, but it is more pronounced in China. In the United States, the per-capita personal income of the wealthiest state (Massachusetts' $82,475) was less than twice that of the poorest state (Mississippi's $45,438) in 2021.[6] In China, it is close to four times (Shanghai's CNY 78,027 vs. Gansu's CNY 22,026).

What is also unique about the distribution of the income among the 31 mainland provinces is that the vast majority of provinces are below the average, or the median is much lower than the mean. This means that it is skewed to the low end of distribution. The mean is pulled up by several very wealthy provinces. When the pension was solely paid by each state-run enterprise to its own retirees based on their previous salaries, such economic disparities might not pose an issue. Had the pension benefit been tied only to each worker's wages over his/her working career in the new pension plan, as it was in the old system, then it is conceivable that a national plan could have accommodated that. It might have been administratively cumbersome in the beginning, but at least it would have been doable. However, that is not how the pension benefit in the new pension system was designed from the start. When the central government established the new pension system in the late nineties, with the basic pension benefit to be paid out of a social pool, it wanted this social pool to achieve two goals: not just old-age insurance but also redistribution, by linking the benefit to the retiree's historical wages and the local average wages. There is also the problem on the contribution side. Even though the contribution is now equal to 16% of wages, it is also within a band, between 60% and 300% of local wages. Thus, the contribution is also tied to local wages.

It is possible that the central government could link the benefits and contributions to the national average wage and thus have a national system. This, however, would run into the problem of wide income disparity across the country. Because of this wide income disparity, workers in wealthy areas would have a smaller pension benefit compared to their pre-retirement wages, and such a design would incite deep resentment in these areas and thus resistance to such a reform. If the contribution was tied to national average wage, then employers in wealthier (poorer) areas would contribute less (more) than under the current system, in contradiction of the goal of redistribution of the current design. Therefore, from the beginning, the central government wanted to avoid the thorny issue of economic disparity when determining pension benefits. The easiest way was to have the local government collect pension contributions and tie the pension benefits to local wages, as presumably, the income disparity is much smaller and thus manageable when the pension benefit determination is limited to a smaller area. Once such a pension benefit design is entrenched, it becomes very difficult to dislodge. In the next chapter on solutions, we discuss possible ways to resolve this tension to achieve the central government's ultimate goal of having a unified national plan.

4.2.2 Disparity in financing

This fragmentation of urban worker pension plans has led to several issues. The first is the sustainability of each local (whether city level or provincial level) pension plan. The sustainability issue discussed earlier in this chapter only deals with the entirety of these plans. However, since each local or provincial government is responsible for its own collection of revenue and disbursement of pension benefits, then there is also a sustainability issue for each of these pension plans. There is significant disparity in the financial health of local or provincial pension plans because of uneven economic development among different regions of the country, leading to mass migration of workers within the country and sustainability issues for individual provincial pension plans, a topic discussed in Chapter 2. While the previous central government's pension fund adjustment mechanism and the current national coordination of provincial pension plans help to some extent, they do not entirely resolve the pension financing disparity among provinces, and thus, the local and provincial governments will still have to provide additional financial support from their budgets to cover the remaining deficits in provinces facing annual funding shortage, putting these local and provincial governments at a disadvantage. Eventually, it is the residents in these areas who will bear the burden since some of the local tax revenues used to pay for pension benefits could have been used to provide better public services. In other words, it is the opportunity cost of government general revenue being used for pension benefits in a local area. In a unified national plan, such burdens will be shared more evenly by everyone in the country, and thus, the opportunity cost will be more evenly spread out across the country.

4.2.3 Inefficiency in governance

The second problem with fragmentation is the inefficiency it generates in at least two areas: administrative cost and potential investment return foregone.

The administrative cost part is easy to understand. With thousands of local pension plans (or even 31 provincial plans), that literally means many duplicative agencies set up with similar responsibilities, such as collecting revenue, maintaining records, investment, and benefit disbursement. Such administrative costs will either have to come out of government's general budget or out of pension plan budgets, resources that otherwise could be used to pay for pension benefits.

This administrative inefficiency pales against the potential loss of investment income. With cumulative balances scattered among many local or provincial plans, each plan's cumulative balance, if there is one, will be relatively small. Such balances are supposed to be invested to earn return to pay for future benefits. A small balance, however, creates two problems for investment. First, the overhead cost will be higher if the pension plan has to hire its investment team to manage the investment. Second, a small balance makes it more difficult to construct an efficient investment portfolio to achieve a higher return while lowering the risk. In reality, due to the difficulty of investing for small balances, many plans simply invest the balance in low-yield bank deposits and government debt. Therefore, on average, the returns on the investment of these balances tend to be lower than those for enterprise annuity funds and the NSSF.

Two recent developments have mitigated this problem to some extent. First, the central government required all provinces to centralize local pension plans into one provincial plan by the end of 2021. Thus, instead of thousands of local plans, we now have 31 provincial plans. A larger provincial pool has an additional advantage over smaller local pools when it comes to investment. For a local plan, it is entirely possible that the money may be needed soon in the future to pay for benefits, and thus, it can only be invested in short-term securities that will generate low returns. For a larger pool, it is more likely that some portion of the pool will not be needed soon and can be invested over a longer period. The second development is that the provinces now can entrust their balances to the NSSF for investment to take advantage of the NSSF's investment expertise. However, this process is still unfolding slowly. As mentioned in Chapter 2, as of 2021, only about 28% of the national balance was entrusted to the NSSF for investment. It is possible that many provinces are still in the process of centralizing the balances of all their local pension plans and thus do not have access to the balances that they can entrust to the NSSF. Thus, the potential loss of investment income is still fairly significant in the near future.

4.2.4   *Migrant workers*

The fragmentation of pension plans, whether at the local or provincial level, has also left millions of migrant workers without the traditional pensions available to urban enterprise workers, as a result of China's unique household registration system.

After the implementation of the open and reform policy in China, with job opportunities opening up in urban areas, hundreds of millions of farmers left rural areas to seek job opportunities in the cities, creating the largest labor force migration in the world. These farmers seeking better wages are called migrant workers. In 2021, there were 292 million migrant workers, accounting for 39% of the people with employment. In any other country, these migrant workers could settle down in the cities where they find jobs and be a part of the local communities. In China, the vast majority of them could not because of the household registration system. Therefore, most of them did not stay in the same city for very long. They either moved to other parts of the country or eventually moved back to their hometowns when they were no longer able to work. In addition, rural migrant workers in urban areas are generally not covered by the public pension plans for urban enterprise workers. Participation is allowed but not compulsory. Both employers and rural migrant workers are reluctant to join because joining entails higher labor costs for employers, and migrant workers are more interested in immediate wages than in pensions decades later. More critically, their high mobility across regions impedes participation. Many of them do not stay in one area for more than 15 years, and thus, they do not qualify for local pension benefits. Had there been a national pension plan, such mobility would not have been an issue. Figure 4.6 gives the percentage of migrant workers covered by the basic pension plans from 2008 to 2017 (reporting on the coverage of migrant workers was discontinued after 2017 by the MOHRSS).

Even though the percentage of migrant workers covered by the basic plans has been increasing slightly from year to year, doubling in ten years between 2008 and 2017 from about 11% to 22%, the coverage was still very low. For comparison, close to 70% of urban workers were covered by the basic pension plans in 2017. Because of this low coverage, most migrant workers participate in the pension plan for urban and rural residents, rather than the pension plan for urban workers, even though they may have worked in various urban areas

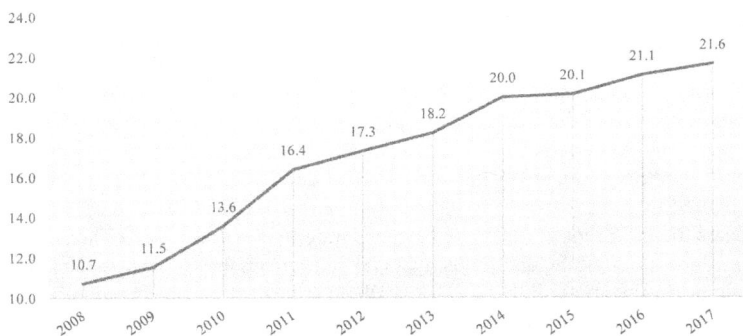

Figure 4.6 Percentage of Migrant Workers Covered by Pension Plans for Urban Workers (%)

Source: MOHRSS annual bulletins.

for more than 15 years. As can be seen in the description of pension benefits in Chapter 2, the average benefit of the plan for urban and rural residents is much lower than that of the plan for urban workers. Therefore, migrant workers are at a severe disadvantage. If the number of migrant workers were small, then such a disadvantage would not have mattered as much in the broad public pension world.

As it was aware of this disadvantage for migrant workers, the Chinese government issued a notice, titled the "Temporary Measure to Link the Urban and Rural Pension Systems" in 2014, to allow migrant workers to switch between two plans, the plan for urban and rural residents and the plan for urban enterprise workers. A migrant can move his/her contributions to his/her individual account in a plan for urban workers to his/her individual account in a plan for urban and rural residents, and these contributions will count towards the minimum 15-year contribution requirement to qualify for the benefits distributed from the latter plan. If he/she contributes to the individual accounts of both plans at the same time, only the contribution to the individual account within the plan for urban workers will count, and his/her contributions to the individual account within the other plan will be returned.

4.3   Challenge 3: Unbalanced pension system

The third challenge for the Chinese pension system is the lopsided dependence on the first pillar of a pension system for the vast majority of people. As discussed briefly in the introduction to this book, the World Bank suggested in 1994 a three-pillar pension system: the first pillar being the public pension, the second pillar being an employer-provided pension, and the third pillar being a self-financed individual retirement account. The main purpose of such a three-pillar system is to spread out the burden of providing financial security in retirement so that no one, the public/government, the employer, or the individual, will be overburdened with the responsibility of providing an adequate pension in retirement in terms of reaching a sufficient replacement ratio. As can be seen from the description of pension plans currently existing in China, the third pillar of individual retirement accounts is nonexistent in China. Only civil servants and a small fraction of urban enterprise workers are currently covered by the second pillar. Therefore, the first pillar of the public pension bears the full brunt of financing pensions in retirement for most of the people in China, thus putting enormous financial pressure on the public pension plans and governments at all levels. This is all the more worrisome when the public pension plans face long-term funding shortages, and the replacement ratio of public pension benefits has also been declining as a result of that.

This unique aspect of the Chinese pension system is even more evident when compared to the U.S. overall pension system. Table 4.2 presents a comparison of the composition of pension assets in China and the United States in 2021.

Table 4.2 Comparison of U.S. and Chinese Pension Assets in 2021

	United States	*China*
First pillar	Social Society: $2.85 trillion	Urban workers plan: CNY 5.26 trillion; Urban and rural resident plan: CNY 1.14 trillion; Total: CNY 6.4 trillion
Second pillar	Private employers: $13.1 trillion State and local government employers: $9.9 trillion Federal government employer: $4.6 trillion Total: $27.6 trillion	Enterprise annuity: CNY 2.61 trillion Occupational annuity: CNY 1.79 trillion Total: CNY 4.4 trillion
Third pillar	Individual retirement accounts: $13.2 trillion	Nonexistent

Source: U.S. Federal Reserve, Financial Accounts of the United States.

It is obvious from the table that while the asset value of China's first pillar is somewhat comparable to that of the United States, the asset values of the other two pillars are not comparable at all. As a matter of fact, at least in terms of assets, the other two pillars dominate the pension system in the United States. Thus, on average, the financing of pension burden is shared more evenly among these three pillars. It should be emphasized here that such numbers are for the whole country. This does not mean that every family in the United States has equal access to these pools of retirement funds. There is still significant variation among different socioeconomic classes in the United States. For example, low-income families, who have very limited resources to set aside funds in individual retirement accounts, or who work in menial jobs that do not provide occupational pension benefits, still mostly rely on Social Security as their primary source of income in retirement. According to a survey of the Social Security Administration, one in four older Americans rely on social security benefits for at least 90% of their income (Dushi, Iams, and Trenkamp, 2017).

It should be acknowledged that this pension system in the United States was established decades ago, and workers in the United States have the U.S. financial markets (both the stock and bond markets) as well as the international financial market available to them, which allow them gradually to build up assets in their retirement portfolio over a long period. Still, the U.S. government has had to pass laws to encourage employers and individuals to set up retirement accounts to invest for the long term to take advantage of the opportunities these financial markets present. Given the value of assets in these retirement accounts, it seems that the majority of Americans and employers have just done that, adding significantly more financial security to their retirement.

Notes

1 The United Nations population database is available at https://population.un. org/wpp/.
2 The significant drop in life expectancy in the late fifties was due to a famine that killed millions of people in China.
3 This is based on a report, titled "MOHRSS states that the actual retirement age is around 53", published by the *People's Daily* on June 19, 2012. Available at http:// finance.sina.com.cn/china/20120620/082212359561.shtml.
4 For U.S. life expectancy, see https://u.demog.berkeley.edu/~andrew/1918/figure2. html.
5 There is some evidence of reluctance on the part of local governments to collect the required employer contribution. As discussed in Section 4.1.2, there is widespread noncompliance with the required employer contribution amount. Even though most local governments have been aware of the issue, it seems there has been no concerted effort to crack down on this practice, as the noncompliance has been persistent. This is becoming less of an issue, as more and more provinces now require the tax administration agency to collect pension contributions.
6 See St. Louis Federal Reserve. Per Capita Personal Income by State. Available at https://fred.stlouisfed.org/release/tables?rid=110&eid=257197.

References

Chinese Academy of Social Sciences. 2019. China Pension Actuarial Report 2019–2050. Beijing: China Labor and Social Security Publishing House.
Dushi, Irena, Howard Iams, and Brad Trenkamp. 2017. The Importance of Social Security Benefits to the Income of the Aged Population. *Social Security Bulletin*, 77(2). Available at www.ssa.gov/policy/docs/ssb/v77n2/v77n2p1.html.
Li, Biao. March 13, 2021. Interview with Chinese Academy of Social Sciences International Social Security Research Center Director Zheng Bingwen. *Daily Economic News*. Available at www.nbd.com.cn/articles/2021-0313/1654675.html.
Liu, Changping. 2008. Studies on the Sustainable Development of Chinese Urban Basic Old-Age Insurance System. Beijing: China Social Sciences Press.
Peng, Xiujuan. June 5, 2022. Could China's Population Start Falling? Available at www.bbc.com/future/article/20220531-why-chinas-population-is-shrinking#:~: text=The%20Shanghai%20Academy%20of%20Social%20Sciences%20team%20 predicts%20an%20annual,of%20what%20it%20is%20today.
Wang, Yanzhong. 2019. Editor-in-Chief, China Social Security System Development Report, No. 10. Beijing: Social Sciences Academic Press.
Zhao, Qin, and Haijie Mi. 2019. Evaluation on the Sustainability of Urban Public Pension System in China. *Sustainability*, 11(5): 1418.
Zheng, Bingwen. 2022. Path to and Goal of National Coordination of Basic Pension Insurance for Workers. *Chinese Journal of Population Science*, 2: 2–16.
Zuo, Xuejin. 2013. Designing Fiscally Sustainable and Equitable Pension Systems in China. Paper presented at IMF OMP/FAD Conference in Tokyo. Available at www. imf.org/external/np/seminars/eng/2013/oapfad/pdf/zuo.pdf.

5   Solutions

Our framework of solutions is tied to the challenges discussed in the previous chapter, namely, the sustainability issue, the fragmentation issue, and the one-sidedness of the Chinese pension system.

5.1   Sustainability

The sustainability issue concerns the funding necessary to pay future benefits. As many other countries also face sustainability issues in their public pension plans, the solutions to sustainability are relatively straightforward to propose because invariably, in all these countries that face sustainability issue, the solutions involve increasing revenue, reducing benefits, or a combination of both.

5.1.1   Increasing revenue

There are many ways China can potentially increase revenue for its basic pension plans. Following are the four major possible sources of increased revenue:

- the most important recurring and mandated revenue source is employer contributions to the social pools;
- investment income on the surplus funds in these social pools;
- the regular transfer of funds from government budgets at all levels; and
- the strategic reserve fund, NSSF, with its own central government revenue transfer, transfer of equity shares of publicly listed state-owned enterprises, and investment returns.

5.1.1.1   Increase employer contributions

While increasing the employer contribution rate is certainly a reasonable option to increase revenue into the system, it completely goes against the recent trend in China. As discussed earlier, in 2019, the Chinese government

DOI: 10.4324/9781003091974-5

actually reduced the employer contribute rate from 20% to the current 16%, even though it was fully aware of the forthcoming funding shortage in the pension plan for urban workers. Given that the government has just reduced the contribution rate, it is hard to imagine it will raise it again any time soon. Therefore, this option is pretty much off the table.

It should be acknowledged that even after this reduction, the contribution rate of 24% (employer's 16% plus employee's 8%) of covered wages for the pension plan is still relatively high when compared with OECD countries, as shown in the previous chapter. A high contribution rate creates incentives for employers to cover fewer employees, underreport wages, and stop contributing after a minimum of 15 years, also as shown in the previous chapter. From this perspective, not increasing the employer contribution rate from the current level will likely remain a long-term government policy.

Instead of increasing the contribution rate, a more promising way to raise more revenue is to enforce the current policy more rigorously by reducing the under-contribution of employers. As discussed in the previous chapter, the reported salary base for pension contribution purposes has been much lower than the actual salary base. One relatively easy solution is to have the tax administration agency collect pension contributions instead of the social security agency. It is much easier for the tax agency to verify the accuracy of the actual salary base, as it is the base on which personal income tax is paid. This can generate a substantial amount of new revenue without increasing the contribution rate. Being aware of this relatively easy way to generate more revenue to offset the pension funding deficit, more and more provinces have shifted the responsibility of collecting pension contributions to tax administration agencies, as shown in our case studies in Chapter 3.

Another way to increase revenue without increasing the contribution rate is to increase the years of contribution to the pension plan before a worker can qualify for retirement benefits. In China, you only need to contribute to the pension plan for 15 years to qualify for basic pension benefits. That is too low a bar to qualify for a public pension. Fifteen years of contribution does not generate enough revenue for pension benefits that can last for decades. The benefit formula says that one year of contributions leads to 1% of replacement ratio, and thus, 15 years will lead to a 15% replacement ratio. Thus, it seems that contributing for a minimum of 15 years does cover the pension cost. However, since the local average wage is also part of the base to determine that 1%, it may be higher at the time of retirement than the wage for many people if they stop contributing long before they retire. Therefore, workers can still get a better benefit compared to the benefit just based on their salary alone. In this respect, contributing for a minimum of 15 years may still add to the cost of the pension system. Again, using the U.S. Social Security benefit as an example, even though the law does not say how many years one has to contribute to collect benefit, the benefit formula itself is based on the average of 35 years of wages. Therefore, there should be an increase in the number of years of contribution to qualify for pension benefit to bring more revenue into the system. If workers contribute less than the higher minimum years of contribution required, it does not have to mean that they will not get a benefit at all when they reach retirement age. Pensions can be structured so that there is a discount in the pension benefit received, with the discount multiplied by the number of years less than the higher minimum threshold so that the benefits received can be better aligned with the contributions made. As indicated in the previous chapter, only about 80% of non-retiring participants in the basic pension plan contribute into the plan. An increase in the years of contribution required, say to 25 years, should also bring in a significant amount of new revenue to the system to help with the sustainability issue.

5.1.1.2 *Investment returns on social pool surpluses*

The second source of revenue that can be increased is investment returns on the cumulative balance of basic plans. This will be possible with an eventual provincial pool of balances of all plans administered at the local level. A larger pool has the potential for a more efficient investment strategy that can increase investment returns while reducing risk. More importantly, since 2015, provincial governments can give their balances to the NSSF for investment due to its track record of investment performance since 2000. Given that only 28% of this total fund balance of over CNY 5 trillion was managed by the NSSF at the end of 2021, most of the funds are still invested at the local and provincial levels, likely in bank deposits, generating low investment returns. Therefore, there is a potential to generate a sizable increase in investment income to the basic pension plans if the cumulative balances are properly invested. In comparison, in the U.S., state and local governments' pension funds for their public employees fully invest their assets in well-diversified portfolios, expecting to earn investment income to reduce their current contribution and pay for future pension benefits (Wang and Peng, 2016). The longer it takes for the rest of the balances to be centralized and invested, the less effective this investment strategy will be in terms of generating extra revenue.

In the long run, however, the revenue upside of this option is still somewhat limited. The reason is that all the cumulative balances are projected to be exhausted by 2035, according to the Chinese Academy of Social Sciences (CASS) actuarial valuation of 2019. With no changes made to the benefit side, cumulative balances will increase for a few more years and then start to decline. Thus, any additional investment income can be generated for only a limited period, and thus, it will only make a relatively small dent in addressing the sustainability issue. Besides, even for the surpluses that can be invested, the time horizon for investment will be relatively short, as some of the funds will be needed relatively soon to cover the annual funding deficit. Therefore, such funds can only be invested in relatively safe short-term securities, further limiting the potential for earning long-term higher return.

5.1.1.3   Government subsidy

Government subsidy already accounts for a very large percentage of the annual revenue for the basic pension plans, and this trend is expected to continue with the ageing of the workforce. Since the government is the guarantor of workers' pension benefits, it is ultimately responsible for the financing of pension benefits. That means that in China, general taxes have always served as a backstop for pension benefits. This is one big difference between China and most other countries. For example, in the United States, Social Security benefits are funded entirely by the Social Security payroll tax with no general tax subsidy. The Social Security Board of Trustees is required to project its financing over a 75-year period every year, which can lead to adjustments in benefits and payroll taxes to make the system financially balanced. While such adjustment does not necessarily happen right away, as it requires Congressional approval, it will eventually occur before the program runs out of money to pay for the full benefits promised. In China, it is different. The line between pension contributions and general revenue as a source of revenue for paying pension benefits is far more blurred. Governments at all levels have been using general revenues to pay for some of the benefits for a long time. This partly reflects the nature of the Socialist planned economy in the past. Even after the reform that began in the seventies, governments at all levels still own a very significant portion of the economy of the country. More importantly, many of the current retirees who have never paid into the current pension plans and are now drawing pension benefits used to work for state-run enterprises. It is thus reasonable to expect the governments to pay for their pension benefits in the form of transfers of general revenues to pension plans if the basic pension plans cannot generate sufficient revenue to pay for them.

In that respect, it is not so much whether governments will continue to subsidize the basic pension plans as whether they will have the financial capacity to pay for the escalating deficits in basic pension plans in the coming decades. According to the CASS's 2019 actuarial valuation, the deficit will run to CNY 11 trillion by 2050, not counting the more than CNY 5 trillion in government subsidy already expected. Because the Chinese economy has already entered a slower growth phase of its development, in the vicinity of 5% a year, rather than the double-digit or high single-digit growth rate of the past, government revenue growth should not be much faster than that. It will certainly be slower than the growth rate of the gap between annual pension revenue and pension payment. Thus, even if the government can continue to bridge the funding gap in the basic pension plan, the more important question is what the opportunity cost will be of this unlimited financial support from governments at all levels for the basic pension plans.

5.1.1.4 National Social Security Fund

In essence, the NSSF, as a strategic reserve fund for China's public pension plans, is an extension of the government subsidy, as most of the seed funds in the NSSF have been and will continue to be transferred from the central government's budget, although it has the added benefit of incurring investment income. In other words, the NSSF is a supplement to the annual tax subsidy to the basic pension plans. Therefore, the rationale for government subsidy for the basic pension plan discussed in Section 5.1.1.3 should also apply to the NSSF.

Because of the power of compounding, such investment income over a very long period of time should surpass the seed funds, which was already the case in 2021. Given its track record of averaging 8.3% investment return over a 20-year period between 2001 and 2021, this reserve fund could double in size in about every eight years, if it can maintain this rate of return, and even faster with continuous annual revenue transfers from the central government. It is therefore conceivable that it could grow into a CNY 10 trillion fund by 2035, from the CNY 2.6 trillion fund in 2021. However, two factors may mitigate this expectation of future long-term investment returns similar to the average return realized in the first 20 years of its existence. First, the past 20-year average return was achieved over a period when the Chinese economy still enjoyed very high growth rates on average. However, such sustained high growth rate is no longer expected over the next two decades. If nothing else, the Chinese population started to decline in 2022. Therefore, the average investment return, which broadly tracks the overall economic growth over an extended period, will more likely be lower over the next two decades than that of the two decades between 2000 and 2020. Second, when the NSSF becomes bigger, it will be more difficult for it to identify investment opportunities to earn investment return that is above the market return. Thus, it is possible that the NSSF may not be able to repeat its investment performance over the next two decades.

In relation to the NSSF, the Chinese government has one powerful weapon in combating the looming pension deficit that is not available to most countries, especially countries with a market-based economy. Chinese governments at all levels control a very large portion of the economy, through state-run enterprises, many of which are listed on the stock exchange. According to the State Council (2021), net assets in state-owned enterprises controlled by central and local governments amounted to CNY 76 trillion in 2021. At the end of 2021, there were 1,317 publicly listed state-owned enterprises with a market value of CNY 33.54 trillion, according to the State-Owned Assets Supervision and Administration Commission of the State Council. The central government has already promised to transfer 10% of its stock shares to the NSSF to assist with basic pension plans. The idea is to earn the dividends that come with these shares to generate a steady source of revenue to the NSSF to pay for pension benefits. As long as the state enterprises remain profitable, this stream of revenue should also grow in the future.

In a sense, it is also only fair to use assets controlled by the governments, in the form of state-owned enterprises, to pay for any deficits in pension financing. One big part of the sustainability issue has to do with the legacy debt, stemming from retirees who had not paid into the pension plan before the transition to the current pension system. Since most of them worked for state enterprises and were paid relatively little while they were working, their sacrifice has been transferred into assets now owned by these state enterprises. Therefore, applying some of their profits to pay for the legacy debt is a sound public policy. Potentially, an even large percentage of equity share should be transferred to the NSSF, if the funding shortage persists in the future with all the reform efforts on the revenue side already implemented.

5.1.1.5 Summary

It should be obvious from this discussion of revenue options that no single revenue solution can address the funding shortage alone, short of a permanent increase in the contribution rate large enough to address the funding problem, an option that is off the table from the central government's perspective. Every option helps. However, even collectively, these options will not generate enough funds to cover the funding shortage by 2050, let alone after that, unless governments at all level promise to cover any shortage in the future with revenue transfers, which will impose severe stresses on public finances and also is not sustainable. For example, even if the value of the NSSF funds increases tenfold to CNY 26 trillion in 2050 from CNY 2.6 trillion in 2021, it will still only cover a relatively small portion of the cumulative deficit of CNY 87 trillion in the basic plan by 2050, according to CASS's 2019 actuarial valuation. Therefore, reduction in benefit has to be part of the equation to address the funding shortage.

5.1.2 *Pension benefit reduction*

For pension benefit, the biggest concern is the ageing of population, which is out of the control of the pension system itself. The only major option available to the government in terms of reducing the benefit cost is to change the rule on age eligibility for collecting basic pension benefits.

As discussed in previous chapters, the retirement age is low in China. It is 60 for men and 50 for women (even lower for some hazardous occupations but also higher for women in some professional and management positions). These age requirements were set in early 1950s, when the life expectancy in China was in the mid-forties. With life expectancy now in the late seventies and expected to grow even higher in the following decades, a gradual increase in the age requirement for retirement is all but inevitable. China also stands out in the world in terms of its early age for retirement. Table 5.1 lists the retirement ages in OECD countries.

Table 5.1 Current and Future Retirement Ages for Males and Females in OECD Countries

Country	Current Retirement Age, Male	Current Retirement Age, Female	Future Retirement Age, Male	Future Retirement Age, Female
Australia	66.0	66.0	67.0	67.0
Austria	65.0	60.0	65.0	65.0
Belgium	65.0	65.0	67.0	67.0
Canada	65.0	65.0	65.0	65.0
Chile	65.0	65.0	65.0	65.0
Colombia	62.0	57.0	62.0	57.0
Costa Rica	61.9	59.9	65.0	65.0
Czech Republic	63.7	63.7	65.0	65.0
Denmark	65.5	65.5	74.0	74.0
Estonia	63.8	63.8	71.0	71.0
Finland	65.0	65.0	68.0	68.0
France	64.5	64.5	66.0	66.0
Germany	65.7	65.7	67.0	67.0
Greece	62.0	62.0	66.0	66.0
Hungary	64.5	62.0	65.0	62.0
Iceland	67.0	67.0	67.0	67.0
Ireland	66.0	66.0	66.0	66.0
Israel	67.0	62.0	67.0	62.0
Italy	62.0	62.0	71.0	71.0
Japan	65.0	65.0	65.0	65.0
Korea	62.0	62.0	65.0	65.0
Latvia	63.8	63.8	65.0	65.0
Lithuania	64.0	63.0	65.0	65.0
Luxembourg	62.0	62.0	62.0	62.0
Mexico	65.0	65.0	65.0	65.0
Netherlands	66.3	66.3	69.0	69.0
New Zealand	65.0	65.0	65.0	65.0
Norway	67.0	67.0	67.0	67.0
Poland	65.0	60.0	65.0	60.0
Portugal	65.3	65.3	68.0	68.0
Slovak Republic	62.8	62.7	64.0	64.0
Slovenia	62.0	62.0	62.0	62.0
Spain	65.0	65.0	65.0	65.0
Sweden	65.0	65.0	65.0	65.0
Switzerland	65.0	64.0	65.0	64.0
Turkey	52.0	49.0	65.0	63.0
United Kingdom	66.0	66.0	67.0	67.0
United States	66.0	66.0	67.0	67.0
OECD—Average	64.2	63.4	66.1	65.5

Source: OECD, Pensions at a Glance.

As can be seen, 65 is the most common retirement age in OECD countries, with the average retirement age in OECD currently very close to that. Also noticeable is that many countries are in the process of increasing retirement age in the future so that the average retirement age will increase by two more years, precisely to account for the longer life expectancy and the resultant funding shortage for public pensions. For example, the United States increased its age for normal Social Security benefits from 65 to 67 in the early eighties. This increase happened very gradually over a long period of time. Germany is also increasing its retirement age from 65 to 67 by 2029. The Chinese government certainly thought of this obvious option long time ago. However, each time the consideration made it into the news, it caused widespread backlash. Even in a one-party political system, the government is still wary of the political cost of offending hundreds of millions of urban workers. Although there were certainly some legitimate reasons for worrying how increasing the retirement age might affect the employment rate in China when the workforce was still growing, now with the workforce actually shrinking, that reason no longer holds. Officially, on December 30, 2021, the State Council issued the "Notice on the 14th Five-Year Plan on the Nation's Old-Age Business Development and Ageing Care Services". In it, the State Council explicitly set the goal of gradually increasing the retirement age, although without laying out any details about how this will be achieved. With this goal set in an official notice, it at least means that it is now on the government's agenda to devise a plan to implement it in the near future.

China is also unique in another respect, namely, the ten-year gap in retirement age between men and women. The majority of OECD countries have the same retirement age for both men and women, as Table 5.1 shows. In the handful of countries with an age difference, it is no more than five years. On average, the difference in retirement age between men and women is less than a year. Therefore, this combination of large age gap and low retirement age makes China an outlier in age eligibility for public pension benefit. This poses a problem for the solution of raising the retirement age. While ideally the retirement age of both men and women should be increased to a similar level, say 65, it would mean such a dramatic increase for women that it could be difficult to win the support of half the workforce. A better alternative is to maintain two separate retirement ages after the increase but with a smaller age gap, say from ten years to just five years. This means that it might be possible to raise men's retirement age to 65, which is a fairly common retirement age in the world, and raise women's retirement age to 60. Despite the age gap, it would still mean a ten-year increase in retirement age for women.

As with common international practice, such increases never happen in one fell swoop. They materialize over many years, with the retirement age increased by a few months every year. CASS (Zheng, 2022) conducted an actuarial valuation on how much savings such a scenario could produce if it were implemented in 2022, and the results were quite revealing. It set out the following assumptions: (1) first, women's retirement age increases by four months every year beginning in 2022; and (2) second, when women's retirement age reaches 55 from 50, then both women and men's retirement age will increase by four months every year until women's retirement age reaches 60 and that for men reaches 65. Under such an assumption, non-retiring participants would increase from 276 million in 2020 to 409 million in 2050 vs. 341 million without reform. For retirees, the number will only increase from 106 million in 2020 to 210 million in 2050 vs. 278 million without reform. This means the ratio of contributing participants over retirees will improve to 1.9 vs. 1.2 without reform.

In terms of revenue, it would increase to CNY 24.8 trillion in 2050 vs. CNY 23.6 trillion without reform. The reform would make a more meaningful impact on benefit cost reduction, as expected. The annual pension cost would reduce from CNY 34.91 trillion, or 11.42% of GDP, to CNY 27.9 trillion, or 9.11% of GDP. Therefore, it would significantly improve the sustainability of the pension system. The exhaustion of the total fund balance would be extended for seven years, from 2035 to 2042. The total nominal deficit between 2035 and 2050 would be CNY 86.8 trillion without reform vs. only CNY 15.6 trillion between 2042 and 2050 with the reform, which can easily be addressed by assets in the NSSF alone.

This analysis shows that increasing the retirement age remains the single most impactful option to reduce the pension financing gap in China. The earlier it is implemented, the more positive the impact will be on the sustainability of the system. Along with other means to increase revenue, including the NSSF strategic reserve fund, it is thus possible to address the long-term funding problem in a sustainable way.

5.2   Fragmentation

By the end of 2021, fragmentation of pension plans for urban workers was no longer as serious as it was in the past. Every province was required to unify all local plans within its province. Therefore, instead of thousands of local plans, we now have 31 provincial plans. For the central government, a unified provincial plan, itself a goal that has taken a long time to realize, is an intermediate step towards the ultimate goal of a national unified plan. A national plan will certainly have many benefits. First of all, it will pull all resources together, making for more efficient management, such as in the area of investment. The biggest benefit, however, is that it may encourage more labor mobility, which in the long run is a plus for economic dynamism and growth. You can work in one province for a few years and move to another part of the country for a better job opportunity without worrying about losing pension benefits already accrued, if you work for less than 15 years in any area. This is especially important for migrant workers, who number in the hundreds of millions. Because not many of them stick in one place for many years, they are the ones who tend to lose the most in terms of pension benefits. A national plan will correct this inequity. It will also encourage more workers, especially migrant workers, to participate in a national plan, thus increasing the system's revenue. A larger pension in retirement will provide more financial security for hundreds of millions of people, and thus, they can spend more in retirement. More consumption in the long run is what the Chinese economy needs to grow in a more sustainable and balanced way. Therefore, it will have a long-term positive impact on the Chinese economy.

However, a national plan will be even more difficult to pull off than a provincial plan, for the same reason that it has taken decades to achieve the goal of provincial plan. And as shown in our case study on Guangdong province, it will take at least until 2025 for it to have a truly uniform provincial plan. On the contribution side, it has to do with the band around the average salary. Even the lowest 60% of the national average salary can be pretty high for some provinces with low average salaries. On the benefit side, it also has to do with the dual purposes pension benefit is to serve, old-age insurance and redistribution, and more importantly, the way it is achieved. With a national plan, if the current benefit formula does not change, that means some of the benefit is tied to a national average salary. If the wage disparity within a province is hard to bridge, it is even more difficult to do that at the national level. A national average wage means winners in poorer regions and losers in wealthier ones. It is possible that workers in poorer areas can earn more in pension benefit in retirement than in wages while working if part of the pension benefit is tied to national average wage, resulting in incentives to retire at the earliest age. On the other hand, retirees in wealthier areas may not have enough to support their standard of living prior to retirement, as the national average wage may not support the higher cost of living in wealthier areas. It is difficult to see how a national plan based on the current benefit formula can be achieved to support both goals of the basic pension plan.

To develop a national plan, it is therefore necessary to rethink the benefit formula while preserving the dual goals of old-age insurance and redistribution. First, the pension benefit formula should be delinked from the local (or national) average wages and instead should be based on the worker's historical wages. Then how can the redistributive purpose be achieved? Here, the U.S. Social Security benefit design provides one example. Similar to the Chinese public pension, the U.S. Social Security benefit is also designed to serve dual purposes, old-age insurance and redistribution. To calculate the benefit:

a) First, your lifetime earnings (earned income but not capital income) are converted into a monthly average income based on 35 years of highest earned wages, indexed for inflation. If you work for less than 35 years, then the amount of wage entered will be zero for each of the 35 years in which no income is earned. The wage subject to Social Security tax is capped every year, adjusted for inflation. For example, wages up to $137,700 would be taxed in 2021. This feature is somewhat similar to the Chinese practice, which limits pension contribution to no more than 300% of local average wage.

b) Second, this average monthly income is broken into three brackets. For example, in 2020, these three brackets applied to income from $0 to $960, $960 to $5,785, and $5,785 to the upper limit (as determined by income limit subject to Social Security Tax). The income levels for the three brackets are adjusted for inflation every year. For the income in the first segment, Social Security will replace 90%, and it will replace 32% of the income in the second segment and 15% of the income in the third bracket. Then the benefits in each bracket are added to reach a monthly Social Security benefit.

c) Thus, on average, when your wage goes up, the overall replacement ratio of Social Security goes down. In essence, portions of contributions from higher wages earners are redistributed to support low-wage earners' Social Security benefit. This is redistribution within the Social Security program itself, much like that of the pension plan for urban workers in China, except it is not linked to any local wages.

d) To help out further with low-wage earners, the U.S. federal government also established another program called Supplemental Security Income. It sets a minimum Social Security benefit level every year, adjusted for inflation, so that if anyone's Social Security benefit is below the minimum amount due to lifelong low wages, the federal government will make up the difference with general tax revenues. Since Chinese governments are already subsidizing pension plans with general revenues, they can also redirect such revenues for this purpose, if they want more redistribution to help out workers earning low wages.

Another advantage of a national plan designed like this is that it can be achieved even without the elimination of the deeply entrenched household registration system in China.

Once the benefit formula is changed, the contribution formula will need to be changed as well. It can simply be based on a certain percentage of a worker's wage, without the band, possibly up to a limit.

5.3 Lopsided pension system

The third challenge to the Chinese pension system is the lopsided nature of the system, which relies almost exclusively on public pension (Pillar 1) for pension benefits for the vast majority of people in the country. A more fundamental long-term solution to the public pension funding shortage is to increase the dependence on pension assets in individual accounts managed by individuals instead of governments. Almost three decades after the World Bank (1994) promoted a three-pillar pension system, it has been touted as a model for retirement planning and even explicitly acknowledged by the Chinese government in recent years.

Conceptually, why is an individual retirement account important for China? There are at least three reasons. First, Chinese people are known for exceptionally high savings rate, and most of those savings are with banks. Due to the low yield on bank savings account, such savings' value is gradually eroded due to inflation, and thus, it is not an ideal vehicle for financing retirement decades away. On the other hand, this can also mean that most Chinese people have the funds to invest in individual retirement accounts for the long run. Second, as discussed earlier, China has a large workforce of migrant workers and a large informal economic sector in which wages are difficult to verify, and therefore, the traditional basic pension plans as designed do not serve them well. An individual retirement account with proper incentives to set it up will be a good vehicle for them for retirement planning. Third, as discussed in Chapter 4, the replacement ratio of public pension benefits has been declining and likely will continue to decline in the future due to the worsening financial situation facing public pension plans. Without other forms of funding that can keep up with inflation and wage growth over decades, retirees in the future may not have enough resources to maintain their quality of life. Given the long-term funding shortage and the decreasing replacement ratio of the public pension plan, a move away from this dominance will not only relieve the pressure on the basic pension plans but also help to protect the financial health of retirees.

However, even after experimentation with the first pillar of the public pension for many decades, the second pillar of occupational pension plans still remains relatively small outside the public sector, where the occupational annuity is mandatory. The third pillar is still almost nonexistent at this point. As it was aware of this problem, the Chinese government implemented a pilot program for individual retirement accounts in a few cities in 2018, according to the "Notice on Conducting the Pilot Program of Personal Tax-Deferred Commercial Pension Insurance", issued by the Ministry of Finance, the State Tax Administration, the MOHRSS, the China Banking and Insurance Regulatory Commission, and the China Securities Regulatory Commission. As in the United States, the contribution to the account would be exempt from income tax and tax would be levied only when funds are withdrawn from the account after retirement. However, this program attracted very little interest, and it was quietly dropped. It is not difficult to understand why such a program would not succeed in China now. Individuals need to be incentivized to put money away for decades in a retirement account, and such incentives are typically tied to a country's tax code. The tax incentives come in two ways. First, the contribution is exempt from taxation until funds are withdrawn from the retirement account during retirement, and any early withdrawal is subject to taxation in the year of withdrawal, plus a penalty to discourage early withdrawal before retirement. Second, and more importantly, the investment return is not taxed until it is withdrawn decades later. Due to the power of compounding, the tax-free return can allow the investment value to grow exponentially over several decades. Therefore, over time, the benefit of this second tax exemption from capital gains tax is more valuable than the first one. However, in China, there is no tax, either ordinary income tax or capital gains tax, on capital gains, thus depriving individuals of the most important incentive to invest in an individual retirement account. China, however, does levy personal income tax on investment income, such as interest income and stock dividends.

On April 8, 2022, the State Council issued the "Opinion on Promoting the Development of Personal Pension Fund", the most important development in the process of establishing a nationwide individual retirement account. It set the annual contribution limit to individual retirement account at CNY 12,000 for 2022, with upward adjustment in the future based on economic condition and other factors. In order to put this opinion into practice, on October 26, 2022, the MOHRSS, Ministry of Finance, State Tax Administration, China Banking and Insurance Regulatory Commission, and China Securities Regulatory Commission issued the "Implementation Measures on Individual Retirement Funds"; and then on November 3, 2022, the Ministry of Finance and the State Tax Administration issued the "Bulletin on Personal Income Tax Policy Related to Individual Retirement Funds". Between these two rules, individual retirement accounts have finally been established in China, another major policy achievement in the long process of establishing a modern pension system in China. The major provisions of these two rules are as follows:

- The annual contribution limit in 2022 is CNY 12,000, subject to increase in the future.
- Accounts can be set up with a commercial bank, and the individual determines the investment products.
- Once a person reaches the age to collect pension benefit, he/she can withdraw funds from the individual retirement account.
- Once the individual passes away, the funds in his/her individual retirement account can be inherited.
- The annual contribution is exempt from personal income tax, which is based on the person's total income. However, the annual withdrawal from the account in retirement is not considered part of a person's total income, and it is subject to a 3% tax rate.

Of all the provisions, the most important one is tax policy regarding contribution to and withdrawal from the individual retirement account, as this is the main policy tool a government has in encouraging people to save for retirement on a voluntary basis. In this case, the Chinese government took both similar and unique steps to achieve this purpose. The familiar step is that the contribution is exempt from personal income tax. Since the contribution is part of a person's total income subject to tax, the tax benefit of this exemption depends on the marginal tax rate facing this individual. The unique aspect of Chinese tax policy is that the annual withdrawal from the account, regardless of the amount, is subject to a uniform 3% tax rate, even if this person may face a higher marginal tax rate due to overall higher income. To understand the tax incentives embedded in these rules, we need to discuss some key features of China's personal income tax structure briefly.[1] These key features are as follows:

- Annual labor income under CNY 60,000 is exempt from taxation. Amounts above that are subject to the following tax rates (Table 5.2):

Table 5.2 China's Personal Income Tax Brackets

Taxable Income	Tax Rate
0 to 36,000	3%
36,000 to 144,000	10%
144,000 to 300,000	20%
300,000 to 420,000	25%
420,000 to 660,000	30%
660,000 to 960,000	35%
Over 960,000	45%

- Some expenses can also be used to reduce the amount of labor income subject to taxation, such as contributions to the basic pension plan, health insurance contributions, mortgage interest, and rental payments.
- Investment income, including interest income, stock dividends, and rental income on investment properties, is subject to a uniform tax rate of 20%.

Following are the two main tax benefits of the individual retirement account as currently designed:

- The amount of tax benefit primarily depends on the marginal tax rate that an individual faces. For someone facing the highest marginal tax rate of 45%, the contribution of CNY 12,000 amounts to a tax deduction of CNY 5,400. At the time of withdrawal, this CNY 12,000 is subject to a tax rate of 3%, meaning this person will have a net tax saving of just over CNY 5,040 on this contribution alone, not counting the tax savings on investment income earned. However, for someone facing a marginal tax rate of 3% at the time of contribution, the net tax saving is minimal.

- A major tax benefit for everyone contributing to the retirement account, regardless of the marginal tax rate he/she faces, is the difference in tax rate on investment income inside and outside the account. As the main purpose of this account is to invest for retirement in the distant future, the tax rate on investment income is of critical importance. For investment income earned outside this account, the tax rate is 20%. For income inside this account, the tax on investment income is not only deferred, allowing the investment income to grow at a faster rate, but it is also levied at a much lower rate of 3% when the investment income is withdrawn. The deferment and the tax rate differential of 17 percentage points can be viewed as the major incentives the Chinese government has provided for this retirement account as currently designed.

It should also be noticed that such tax benefits primarily go to high-income earners. Since the first CNY 60,000 is exempt from taxation, and given other exemptions, a person needs to make over CNY 100,000 a year to face a marginal tax rate of over 3% to receive more meaningful net tax savings. In comparison, the average annual salary of a private-sector employee in urban areas in 2021 was CNY 106,837, according to China's National Bureau of Statistics. For a worker with an average salary, it will also be difficult to put away CNY 12,000 in a year to take full advantage of the tax benefit on investment income. Therefore, the majority of workers in China will not see much tax benefit from this retirement account.

Since the policy for establishing individual retirement accounts has only been recently published, it remains to be seen to what extent it will incentivize people to invest for the long term in their personal retirement accounts. As discussed, the incentive is relatively weak for workers with low to average annual salaries, and if the Chinese's government's objective is to encourage more voluntary long-term investment for retirement, the current design may not work for this group of people, who arguably need more help than those in the high-income group. For this group of people, instead of a tax exemption, a better approach is simply for the government to provide a matching fund for individual contributions. The advantage of this method is that the benefit is transparent, immediate, and measurable for individuals, thus providing a strong incentive for contribution.

Note

1 The details of China's personal income tax are laid out in the "People's Republic of China Personal Income Tax Law", available at the website of the State Tax Administration. Available at www.chinatax.gov.cn/chinatax/n810219/n810744/n3752930/n3752974/c3970366/content.html.

References

State Council. October 21, 2021. Comprehensive Report on the Management of State-Owned Assets in 2020. Available at http://www.npc.gov.cn/c2/c30834/202110/t20211025_314313.html.

Wang, Qiushi, and Jun Peng. 2016. An Empirical Analysis of State and Local Public Pension Plan Funded Ratio Change, 2001–2009. *American Review of Public Administration*, 46(1): 75–91.

World Bank. 1994. Averting the Old Age Crisis: Policies to Protect the Old and Promote Growth. Available at https://documents1.worldbank.org/curated/en/973571468174557899/pdf/multi-page.pdf.

Zheng, Bingwen. 2022. How Does Delaying Retirement Affect Pension Benefits? SSL Working Paper Series. Chinese Academy of Social Sciences. Available at www.etk.fi/en/work-and-pensions-abroad/international-comparisons/retirement-ages/.

6 Conclusion

Over a 40-year period, roughly between 1980 and 2020, China built up a nationwide pension system that is available to just about every adult over the age of 16, literally from scratch. It covered about 1.03 billion people in 2021, which is a major achievement in and of itself in a country of 1.4 billion people in 2021. This Chinese pension system, while sharing some similarities with pension systems in other countries, has also shown some unique features that reflect its stage of economic development, political system, rural/urban divide, and governance structure. In this final chapter, while summarizing the main features of Chinese pension system that highlight these similarities and differences, we focus mainly on the lessons drawn from our case study on the Chinese pension system.

6.1 Lesson 1: Design of public pension benefit in an economy with a large informal sector

The network of three Chinese public pension plans essentially offers two types of pension benefits. One is based on wages, for urban enterprise workers and public-sector employees, funded by employer and employee contributions. The other, for everyone else, is a combination of a base pension benefit, which is determined and funded entirely by governments and payments from individual retirement accounts. While this two-track benefit system can be traced back to some historical factors, such as the unique household registration system established in China in the 1950s, it also reflects China's current phase of economic development. Despite the fast modernization of its economy since the late seventies, the informal sector, including farmers and migrant workers, still accounts for a very large part of the workforce and the economy. Thus, China's design for urban and rural resident pension plans serves as a model for any country with a large informal sector in which wages are hard to verify with flexible employment. As Chapter 2 shows, more than half of the people covered by the Chinese pension system are actually in this plan, an indication of the scale of this informal sector in China, and the importance of this plan in extending public pension coverage to the majority of people in China. There are, however,

DOI: 10.4324/9781003091974-6

two main issues with the current design of this pension benefit in China. First, the base amount set by the central government is very low. It is not clear how this base amount was arrived at or what policy objective it is designed to serve. While local government can add to this base amount, this creates its own set of problem, namely, inequity in pension benefit across different regions of China. Second, based on the data in Chapter 2, the level of average contribution to individual accounts, a prerequisite for receiving this base pension benefit from the government, is very low, leading to a very small account balance. It seems that most people contribute at a level that is at the lower end of the range recommended by the government, just so that they can be eligible for the base pension payment. This indicates that most people in this pension plan treat this as a social welfare program rather than a retirement program.

In light of this, the design for this plan can be changed to achieve the main objective of this pension plan doubling as a welfare program, which is to meet some minimum level of financial security in retirement. A good measure for that can be a country's poverty level. Therefore, the base pension amount set and funded by the central government should be increased. For the individual account, one required contribution level is probably sufficient, although it can be set at a level higher than the current minimum level. The result is that the sum of the base pension amount funded by the government and the payout from the individual account should put the pensioner above the poverty level. The government can decide how the total payment should be split between the base pension payment and individual account payout. Such a design not only addresses the welfare orientation of this public pension plan but also requires personal responsibility in pension planning, which is also a feature of the current plan design. Local governments can also add to the base pension to account for the higher cost of living in some regions.

6.2 Lesson 2: Establishing a national public pension plan

One unique feature of the Chinese public pension system is its fragmentation, especially the fragmentation of public pension plans among its 31 mainland provinces. While there were historical reasons for such a setup in the beginning, it has led to a host of problems decades later, as discussed in Chapter 4. Thus, the second lesson from this case study is to establish a national plan based on employment and wages, in addition to the public pension plan discussed in Section 6.1, to cover as many people as possible in the beginning. While certain occupations and geographical areas can be carved out for separate pension plans, such fragmentation should be kept to a minimum. A national plan has multiple advantages. The biggest one by far is that it encourages labor mobility. No one needs to be worried about losing accrued pension benefits when switching jobs and/or moving to a different part of the country. In the long term, labor mobility is not only beneficial to an individual's career but also conducive to the overall economic and productivity growth, as labor is chan-neled to where it is needed most. A second advantage, which is related to the first advantage of labor mobility, is that it encourages more participation in the public pension program since any income earned in any place will be counted towards the income base to calculate the final pension benefit. The third major advantage is that it is administratively more efficient, due to the lower over-head cost and also more efficient investment management. A fourth advantage is that it eliminates the pension burden on local governments, meaning that the burden of pension funding will be evenly spread across the entire coun-try since it is now the responsibility of the central government. Again, this is a reflection of labor mobility. Local government should not be responsible for the aftermath of labor movement in terms of pension financing. This also removes one factor that can lead to competition among local governments, which can be detrimental to the economic well-being of the entire country.

Based on the Chinese experience, to establish a national plan, the pension benefit should also be based on a person's own historical wages, rather than partly based on his/her own historical wages and partly based on some other measure of wages, such as national average wages, as there can be substantial variation around the national average. If a government's objective is for the public pension also to serve a social welfare function, in terms of support-ing people with lifelong low wages in their retirement, this objective can be accomplished in two ways. First, a formula can be designed so that people at the low-income level can receive a pension that will replace a higher per-centage of their pre-retirement wages. While high-income earners will still receive a larger pension benefit, the replacement ratio will be lower than that for low-income earners. This way, high-income earners partially subsidize low-income earners' pension benefits. Second, if designed in such a way and the pension benefit of some low-wage earners is still very low, say lower than the poverty level, then the government will need to create a separate welfare program to pay for the difference. That subsidy will have to come out of a government's budget. This essentially means that the burden of providing an adequate pension benefit to low-wage earners is shared between the public pension plan itself and the government. One advantage of such a design is that the financial obligations of both the pension plan and the government can be identified and planned for, and it will not be too onerous for either of them.

6.3   Lesson 3: Addressing funding shortages in the public pension plan

China's public pension plan shares one common problem with public pension plans in almost all other countries, namely, the worsening funding situation due to population ageing. While the Chinese government anticipated this long ago, and it has taken some steps to address it, such as establishing the strategic reserve fund, the NSSF, and slowing the growth rate of pension benefits for retirees, it has not yet taken any steps to address, in a more fundamental way, the funding gap that will escalate further in the future. One reason is that the Chinese public pension plans are heavily subsidized by government general revenue, rather than exclusively funded by dedicated pension contributions from employers and employees, a reflection of the unique nature of the Chinese political and economic systems. What is more unusual is that there is no law or regulation specifically stipulating the extent to which government general revenue should make up for the deficit in the public pension plan. With such an open-ended commitment, the pension deficit can be covered for many years to come, thus reducing the urgency to tackle the problem as early as possible. A major drawback of such an open-ended commitment is that it is achieved at the expense of other vital public services since fiscal resources will have to be shifted from these services to pay for the pension deficits.

Thus, the third lesson is that once a long-term problem is identified, government officials in positions to adopt policy should find solutions to address it as soon as possible. For public pensions, the long-term problem facing most countries is the ageing of the population due to longer life expectancy and lower fertility rates. As a result of actuarial valuation, a long-term funding gap can be determined, and policymakers should identify and adopt policies to address the funding problem. Such solutions invariably involve either raising more revenue or reducing pension benefits. More likely, it will be a combination of both so that neither revenue increase nor pension decrease will be too onerous. Typically, once the problem is known, then the longer it takes to adopt sensible policies to address the problem, the more painful the final solutions will be, meaning that more revenue will need to be raised and more benefits will need to be cut. In China, since increasing the contribution rate is no longer an option, an obvious solution is to reduce pension benefits by increasing the retirement age. The retirement age should have been raised in China a long time ago. Since such an increase in retirement age will need to happen slowly over a very long period of time, the earlier it starts, the more effective the solution will be in addressing funding shortages. Not increasing the retirement age does not necessarily mean that retirees' benefits will be protected. As can be seen in China, because of the funding shortage, retirees' benefits have been increased at a much slower rate in recent years than in the past. As a result, the replacement ratio of pension benefits has been gradually declining. This is an indirect reduction in pension benefits for Chinese retirees, although it is more difficult to see and thus less objectionable.

6.4   Lesson 4: Dealing with legacy pension debt

The effect of population ageing in China on public pension financing is further exacerbated by the legacy pension debt. Any public pension plan, when first established, will incur legacy debt if funded on a PAYGO basis. In China, this legacy debt, which was never properly accounted for by the government, not only was large initially but also has been growing due to the increase in life expectancy. Thus, the fourth lesson from this case study on China is that during the transition to a modern public pension plan, it is important to figure out the legacy debt, through actuarial valuation and then, more importantly, to come up with a way to pay off this legacy debt over a reasonable period. What is not advisable is to muddle through in the hope that somehow, it will eventually be resolved by a future generation of workers who will contribute to the pension plan. Without proper accounting and financing methods, such legacy debt will have the potential to grow over time and thus become more burdensome for future generations. It can keep growing because people will live longer and the debt not paid off will also keep growing due to accrued interest. In China, this legacy debt is partially paid off by the balance in individual accounts, government revenue transfers, and higher employer contribution rates than would otherwise be necessary. This leads to empty individual accounts, the balance of which continues to grow with notional interest promised by the government.

One effective way to pay off the legacy debt is for the national/central government to issue a bond, with the proceeds deposited into a national pension fund to pay off the legacy debt. As the debt is issued by a national government, the interest rate on the debt should be reasonably low and more affordable. The cost is under control and predictable. Once the central government makes regular debt payments, which will not increase over time due to the fixed interest rate on the bond, then the debt will be on a steady trajectory to be eliminated in the future. Better yet, since the debt proceeds deposited into the pension plan can also be invested, as such funds will not be used up for many years to come, if the investment return is higher than the interest rate on the debt, that will be another potential benefit of this approach. In essence, this approach spreads the cost of legacy debt over the next generation of taxpayers, and the pension contribution rate over the next generation also does not need to be set so high to generate extra revenue to pay off the legacy debt. Since workers contributing to pension plans in the next generation will also be taxpayers in the next generation, they will still bear the burden of paying off the legacy debt. The advantage of this approach, however, is that the cost is no longer borne by the higher pension contribution rate alone. As seen in China's case, a higher pension contribution rate leads to noncompliance with pension contributions and disincentives to join the public pension plan. Since the contribution rate is already higher than it should be, there is no room for further increases in the contribution rate to address the looming funding shortage as a result of population ageing.

6.5 Lesson 5: A more balanced pension system

Another unique feature of Chinese pension system that goes beyond the public pension plans is the lopsidedness of its pension system, especially in comparison with that in the United States. In particular, there is the absence of the third pillar of individual accounts to support the first pillar of the public pension. Given the decreasing replacement ratio of the public pension, it is up to individuals to secure additional funds in retirement for financial security. Thus, the fifth lesson from this case study is to establish a multi-pillar pension system as soon as possible. While it is absolutely critical to establish the first pillar of public pensions for the general public, especially for people with low incomes throughout their working careers, to ensure some degree of financial security in retirement, the government should also establish a legal framework and tax incentives early on to encourage workers to set up individual retirement accounts to supplement the public pension benefits. This will not only add more financial security in retirement but also diversify retirement portfolios so that if the public pension benefit is reduced due to funding shortages in the future, the retirees will still have their own individual retirement accounts to fall back on so that the replacement ratio of both public pension benefits and individual account withdrawals can remain relatively stable over time. This combination of public pensions and individual retirement accounts also promotes the notion that the responsibility for financial security in retirement should be borne by both the government and individuals. China finally took concrete steps in 2022 to allow individuals to set up personal retirement accounts with some tax incentives. It still remains to be seen how many people will start doing that in the future. In countries where tax incentives are not strong enough to encourage people to set up individual retirement accounts, an alternative is to provide government matching funds for individual contributions. The benefits of such matching funds are that they are transparent, immediate, and measurable. To reduce the cost of the matching fund to the government, the matching level can be tailored to the incomes of individuals, with higher levels of matching for people with lower incomes.

Index

Note: Page numbers in *italic* indicate a figure and in **bold** indicate a table on the corresponding page.

For Product Safety Concerns and Information please contact our EU
representative GPSR@taylorandfrancis.com
Taylor & Francis Verlag GmbH, Kaufingerstraße 24, 80331 München, Germany